Intentionally Living

Monique Loviel

La'Toya Guillory

Shelia Harris

Jakeithia Prejean

Dr. Sharmonia Wimberly

Jessica Harris

MyAsia Obazee

DEDICATION

First and foremost, this book is dedicated to God the true Author of our faith. It is by His wisdom, grace, and divine purpose that this work has come to life. May every word within these pages reflect His love, guidance, and the power of intentional living.

To you, the reader,

This book is also dedicated to your courage, your willingness to take the first step toward the change you've been longing for. By picking up this book, you've already chosen to embrace a life of intentionality, and that decision alone is a testament to your strength and determination.

Your support fills our hearts with joy and reminds us why we were chosen for such a time as this. You were created for a purpose, on purpose, and with purpose. You are uniquely designed to leave a lasting imprint on this earth, and God has given you the grace to walk boldly in your calling.

As you journey through these pages, prepare to be pulled out of stagnation, propelled into purpose, and launched into destiny. Trust the process, lean into the transformation, and know that you are equipped and empowered for everything God has placed before you.

Live Life Intentionally!

With love and gratitude,

The Coaches

Foreward

The voice of the Lord is calling out to the nations, drawing them forth from the structures and patterns of this world. Do not be conformed; instead, be transformed by the renewing of your mind through Christ's revelation. It is time to intentionally live according to His Word in order to align with heavenly purpose and walk in your predestined calling.

Now is the time to see the light and simplicity of His Word, which calls you out of darkness and raises you up as a living sacrifice. You have been called to increase in the heights, depths, and stature of Christ. You are a remnant of God's saviors who live in righteousness and hail from Zion. You were born to be fearless, to live intentionally in the Spirit, to hold forth the gates of excellence, and to understand the times and seasons in which He moves within and through you.

Remember, intentional living is rooted in divine wisdom, understanding, and inspiration from the Holy Spirit. We align with His instructions in order to understand His will and respond to His promptings. God is calling you to be an intentional living stone among others. When you intentionally live with God, you become one with Him.

This book will show you how to intentionally live out your purpose in alignment with God's will.

Shalom.

Joshua Obazee

ACKNOWLEDGMENTS

To all the incredible contributors of the Intentionally Living anthology,

With heartfelt gratitude, I extend my deepest thanks to each of you for being a vital part of this transformative journey. Bringing this anthology to life has been a labor of love, and your dedication, wisdom, and willingness to share your unique voices have made it a resource that will undoubtedly empower and uplift its readers.

You sacrificed your time, energy, and hearts to create strategies and share insights that will help readers navigate life's challenges with clarity and purpose. Your contributions are more than words on a page; they are seeds of transformation, guiding others to live intentionally and embrace the fullness of life.

Thank you for your partnership, your authenticity, and your commitment to making an impact. Together, we've created a work that will inspire and change lives for years to come.

With gratitude and love,

Monique Loviel

TABLE OF CONTENTS

Published, Editing, and Formatting by: La'Toya Guillory

Empowered with Purpose LLC

Email: info@empowered-with-purpose.net

Website: www.empowered-with-purpose.net

Graphics: Monique Loviel,

pivotalimpactcc@gmail.com

Photos: Shelia Harris, Touch of Class Photography

toughofclassphotography2017@gmail.com

FROM DROUGHT TO DELUGE: REVIVING THE SOUL AND FINDING GOD'S REFRESHING IN LIFE'S DRY SEASONS

WRITTEN BY MONIQUE LOVIEL

There are seasons in life when it feels like the heavens have closed and we're walking through a barren wilderness. The vibrant connection we once had with God now feels distant, like a memory fading into the background of our busy lives. Life's storms, sins, past trauma, and even the mundane tasks of everyday living can leave us feeling spiritually drained. We find ourselves in a place where God's presence seems absent, and the spiritual nourishment that once sustained us is nowhere to be found. In moments like these, it's easy to feel alone, as though we're walking this path by ourselves. This is the painful reality of spiritual dryness, a season many of us experience but few talk about openly.

Spiritual dryness often comes quietly, creeping in over time. It might start with distractions, things that pull our attention away from God, and slowly, we drift. Unmet expectations and past hurt create gaps in our hearts that only God can heal, but we often avoid bringing them to Him. As we neglect our relationship with God, the distance grows. We find ourselves asking, "Where is God?" Prayer feels dry, Bible reading lacks revelation, and the heaviness of the world begins to cloud our spiritual vision. Little by little, the spiritual thirst that once drove us to seek God's presence starts to fade.

We don't notice it at first, but eventually, we find ourselves in a place of spiritual desolation, longing for something we can't quite reach. But what if we looked at this season of dryness as more than a struggle? What if we saw it as an invitation, an invitation to go deeper with God than we've ever gone before?

This isn't a period of failure but a chance for growth. A dry season doesn't have to be a dead end; it can be the beginning of a new chapter in our spiritual journey. God's invitation is still there, even when we feel far from Him. It's in these moments of longing and emptiness that God has the opportunity to draw us closer, to reveal parts of His nature we may have missed before.

When we learn to recognize the signs of spiritual dryness, when we acknowledge the distractions, unmet expectations, and wounds that have led us here, we can begin the process of healing. It may not be a quick fix, but God doesn't abandon us in these times. Instead, He longs to pour out His presence like a flood, renewing us in every way. We don't have to stay stuck in the drought; there is hope for restoration. Transitioning from spiritual dryness to spiritual deluge is a journey, but it's one that leads to a refreshing, a renewal that brings us back to the life and peace we've been longing for.

A spiritual deluge is a powerful outpouring of God's presence and blessings, an overwhelming flood of His Spirit that refreshes, renews, and restores our hearts. It is not just a one-time event but a lifestyle, one of constant renewal and overflowing abundance. The term "deluge" suggests a flooding, an outpouring that leaves no area untouched.

It is God's will for humanity to dwell in His presence, and He has created an oasis where we can experience liberty, abundance, and rest. When we align ourselves with God's will, we enter into His divine rest, free from the pressures of life. In this spiritual deluge, God floods our hearts with His Spirit, filling us with peace, joy, and power. His love and presence bring healing, restoration, and the ability to rise above life's struggles with unshakable hope.

Spiritual dryness doesn't happen overnight. It often creeps in gradually until we realize that something is missing, something that was once a constant part of our lives. Here are some common symptoms and effects of spiritual dryness:

- **Lack of Desire for Prayer and Bible Study**: In a dry season, prayer feels like a burden rather than a joy. Bible study no longer feels alive or transformative, but instead, it may feel like a task to check off on a list.

- **Loss of Peace and Joy**: When God's presence is distant, peace and joy are replaced by restlessness and anxiety. We may find ourselves searching for solace in other things, only to come up empty.

- **Frustration and Irritability**: As we feel distant from God, irritability can begin to creep in. Relationships may suffer, and our patience grows thin. We may snap at others or find it difficult to be still and content.

- **Withdrawal from Fellowship**: Isolation is another symptom of spiritual dryness. We may stop attending church or avoid fellowshipping with other believers, feeling disconnected or as though we don't belong.

These symptoms, if left unchecked, can lead to spiritual separation from God, as noted in **Isaiah 59:2**: "But your iniquities have separated you from your God; your sins have hidden His face from you so that He will not hear." (NIV)

There are many factors that contribute to spiritual dryness. Identifying the root causes is essential to moving past it. Here are some potential causes:

- **Sin and Unconfessed Transgressions**: When sin is left unchecked, it creates a barrier between us and God. Psalm 66:18 warns, "If I had cherished sin in my heart, the Lord would not have listened." Repentance is key to restoring intimacy with God. (NIV)

- **Busyness and Distractions**: Life's responsibilities often push spiritual practices aside. Work, family, and other distractions can crowd out our time with God, leading to spiritual emptiness.

- **Unmet Expectations and Disappointment**: When our prayers seem unanswered or life takes unexpected turns, we may grow disillusioned. These feelings of disappointment can contribute to spiritual dryness if we do not seek healing through God's Word and presence.

- **Emotional Trauma and Unhealed Wounds**: Past hurts and unresolved emotional pain can prevent us from drawing near to God. When we neglect to allow Him to heal our wounds, we may experience spiritual depletion.

Spiritual health can be understood through the lens of three zones: the Green Zone, the Yellow Zone, and the Red Zone. The Bible tells us we should cross-examine ourselves, and he will open the eyes of our hearts. God wants us to grow and prosper in every area of our life, especially spiritually. These zones help us assess our spiritual state and understand where we need to focus our efforts to return to God's presence.

- **The Green Zone: Spiritual Vitality and Health**
  The Green Zone represents spiritual health and vitality. Here, prayer feels natural, Bible study brings deep revelation, and we experience a sense of peace and joy. In this zone, we walk in alignment with God's will, finding strength to face life's challenges. We are filled with spiritual vitality.

- **The Yellow Zone: Spiritual Caution and Frustration (7-14 days)**
  The Yellow Zone is a cautionary state. While we're not in full spiritual dryness, we begin to feel the symptoms of depletion. The Yellow Zone encompasses:

  - **The Zone of Drought**: Here, our connection to God feels distant. Prayer is dry, Bible study lacks depth, and we find ourselves spiritually thirsty. This is a time when we must be vigilant to avoid slipping into full dryness.

  - **Frustration and Irritability**: In the Yellow Zone, irritation and frustration start to surface. We become agitated more easily, and our relationships may suffer as a result. The lack of intimacy with God causes us to feel emotionally drained and restless.

- o **Distance from God**: We feel spiritually disconnected, but we aren't yet in a state of complete separation. We may be busy or distracted, but we must actively seek God to prevent moving into the Red Zone.

- **The Red Zone: Spiritual Separation and Crisis (14+ days)**
  The Red Zone represents spiritual crisis and separation. In this zone, we feel distant from God, and our faith begins to falter. The Red Zone includes:

  - o **The Zone of Separation**: This is where the disconnect from God is most pronounced. Prayer seems fruitless, and worship feels meaningless. Doubt and despair take hold, and we question God's goodness and presence.

  - o **Crisis of Faith**: We may begin to experience doubts about God's promises, His love for us, or even the reality of our faith. We may feel abandoned and forsaken.

  - o **Separation and Loss**: If left unchecked, the Red Zone can lead to a deeper spiritual fall. The longer we stay here, the more we risk losing our sense of purpose and connection with God.

The Story of David and His Men: Spiritual Depletion After War

Let me share with you a story about David and His Men returning back from war just to find their homes raided and families taken captive. The Bible tells the story of David and his men in 1 Samuel 30. After returning from battle, they found their city, Ziklag, raided and their families taken captive.

David and his men were spiritually and emotionally depleted. Their initial response was to weep until they had no strength left. They were devastated, frustrated, and angry.

"When David and his men came to Ziklag, they found it destroyed by fire and their wives and sons and daughters taken captive. So David and his men wept aloud until they had no strength left to weep" (1 Samuel 30:3-4, NIV).

The grief and frustration were palpable, and David's men even turned against him, speaking of stoning him. This is a clear example of the Yellow Zone, spiritual depletion, frustration, and irritability leading to relational strain.

But David didn't remain in the Yellow Zone. "But David found strength in the Lord his God" (1 Samuel 30:6, NIV). Instead of giving in to despair, David turned to God for strength and guidance. God instructed David to pursue the raiders, and he recovered everything that had been taken, even more than he had lost. Through his reliance on God, David transitioned from the Yellow Zone into a time of spiritual deluge.

One day, I broke down in my car, feeling depleted, drained, and distant from God. So many things were happening within two weeks, work, relationships, church, business, and school. I had recently left my church, and work had become overwhelmingly stressful, not so much because of the workload, but because the environment was toxic and non-conducive to my well-being. I felt myself slowly drifting away from God. At first, I stopped praying daily, but then it became every other day, and eventually, I only prayed once in a blue moon. I became easily distracted by my projects, the busyness of work, family, and school, all of which pulled me away from studying the Word.

Normally, I can recognize when I'm entering a dangerous spiritual zone. When I sense myself reaching the "yellow zone," I press into God through prayer, and the Holy Spirit resuscitates me bringing me back to prayer, study, and focus. But this time, I had surpassed the yellow zone and entered the red zone. To be honest, my spirit was dying. I felt like a walking zombie, which ultimately led to my breakdown in the car. I had been delivering materials for work to a sponsor, and as I pulled away, I suddenly found myself crying uncontrollably. I pulled into another parking lot, tears streaming down my face, and cried out, "LORD, help me!"

I began to rant and pour out my heart to God, being completely transparent about how I was feeling; nonexistent. "No one sees that I need help. No one sees that my soul is in tears." But I firmly believe that God responds to our transparency, not just our ranting. Being open with Him shows our willingness to be vulnerable and surrender, just as Job did, just as Jesus did in the Garden of Gethsemane.

Suddenly, I pulled myself together and drove home. Later that night, a friend of mine, who is a trauma coach, reached out to me. She told me that God had placed me on her heart, and she felt led to call. I broke down again, sharing everything I had been feeling. She began to minister to me, reminding me that God was dealing with the matters of my heart and soul. What I was feeling was part of the process. I had become so consumed with everything else that I was using it to mask my pain, but the burden had become too heavy for my spirit to bear. In other words, I needed to heal, but that required changes on my part, first, by accepting responsibility, and second, by setting boundaries. I remember telling her, "I'm tired of being there for everyone else, building their projects, businesses, ministries, personal development, what about me? Where is my help? Where is my team?"She quietly responded, **"How can God build you a team when you haven't allowed Him to build you?"** That struck a chord. It hit me hard.

Avoidance is a trauma response. Typically, I deal with trauma by keeping myself busy with projects, until I lose interest and move on. She prayed for me, and the next day, I changed the way I prayed. Instead of focusing on my struggles, I began praying about the **Kingdom opposite** of what I was going through. I created prayer points to incorporate into my daily prayers. I slowly began pacing myself back to God. He had never left me, I had left Him.

In any relationship, you have to work on yourself to build something strong. The same goes for your relationship with God, except that you work on yourself **with Him**. He has given us the greatest Counselor, the Holy Spirit.

As I continued pressing into God through prayer, study, and worship, I found myself growing closer to Him again. Just like in therapy, I focused on one or two areas at a time, asking God to help me heal. I went on a fast to break every dead weight and barrier hindering my spiritual growth and relationship with Him. Just as it takes **21 days to form a new habit, it takes 21 days to break one.** I felt different. I felt a wave of refreshing sweep over me. Even as I write this, I feel the wind of peace surrounding me, an Edenic experience, like when Adam walked with God in the cool of the day. That was my experience. The Holy Spirit hovered over me, resuscitating me back to life.

Talitha Kumi—"Little girl, arise." I arose out of the red zone, the dead zone. I crossed over the yellow zone, where distractions tried to pull me back, but I stayed focused. I messed up a few times, but I got back up, until I made it to the green zone. The spiritual deluge had come, not just to deliver me out of the red zone, but to help me survive the exit, because there is warfare in the crossover through the yellow zone. Yet, I pressed on to thrive in the green zone.

It is important to understand that God has not only made this deluge available to us, but He has also equipped us with the power and authority to access it. Through the sacrifice of Jesus Christ, we have been given authority over the things that would attempt to deplete our spirits, sin, depression, anxiety, illness, generational iniquity, and all forms of adversity. Just as Jesus told the man who was paralyzed, "Pick up your mat and walk" (John 5:8), we too have the authority to pick up our mats—the burdens and chains of our past and walk into the freedom and victory God has promised.

We no longer need to remain in a state of spiritual or emotional paralysis, weighed down by the things that have held us back. The power of the Holy Spirit that raised Jesus from the dead is available to us to overcome these obstacles.

The Old Testament prophet, Ezekiel was commanded by God to prophesy to the dry bones in the valley, and as he spoke God's Word, the bones came together and were covered with flesh (Ezekiel 37:1-10). After the bones came together, God commanded Ezekiel to prophesy to the breath (or wind), asking it to come from the four winds and breathe life into the slain. When Ezekiel obeyed, the breath entered the bodies, and they stood up as a vast army. This powerful moment shows us that God's Spirit is able to revive even the most hopeless of situations. We, too, can prophesy to the wind of God's Spirit, calling it to return to us and breathe life into every dry, broken place in our lives. No matter how impossible it may seem, God has the power to resurrect what seems dead. He has the ability to heal the wounded heart, restore broken relationships, and transform our circumstances.

When we find ourselves in spiritual drought or emotional distress, we can trust God to lead us to the still waters that will refresh our souls (Psalm 23:2). The still waters of God's presence are where we find peace, rest and spiritual nourishment. It is in these quiet, sacred moments that we allow His Spirit to replenish and restore us. God's desire is for us to be like a tree planted by the waters, bearing fruit in every season, with our leaves never withering (Jeremiah 17:8). God's vision for us is not to remain in a dry, barren land but to become a well-watered garden, flourishing in every area of our lives.

He promises that those who delight in Him will be like trees planted by streams of water, whose leaves will never wither and who will bear fruit in their season (Psalm 1:3). This imagery of a well-watered garden speaks of a life continually nourished by God's presence, where His river of life flows freely through us, bringing peace, joy, and abundance.

Imagine yourself walking in the oasis of Eden, where the cooling breeze of God's presence is ever near. Picture yourself walking beside streams of living water, feeling the refreshing touch of the Holy Spirit as He replenishes your soul. This is the life that God desires for you, a life of continual refreshing and renewal, where you are fully alive in Him.

The water that flows from His throne is not just for a moment but for eternity, a fountain of life that never runs dry (Revelation 22:1-2).

In the Garden of Eden, God created a paradise where His presence was tangible, where Adam and Eve walked in close communion with Him. This garden was lush, full of life, and surrounded by streams of water. It was a place where humanity could experience the fullness of God's blessings—peace, abundance, rest, and joy. When sin entered the world, humanity was cast out of Eden, and we lost the direct access to God's presence that we once had. But through Jesus Christ, we have been granted a way back to the garden. He is the Way, the Truth, and the Life (John 14:6), and through Him, we have been reconciled to God and invited to dwell in His presence once again.

As believers, we are called to return to the oasis of Eden, the place where God's presence fills every part of our lives. In this oasis, we are spiritually replenished and restored, just as the Israelites were when they found the refreshing waters of Elim in the desert (Exodus 15:27). We are invited to live in the abundance of His presence, to drink from His river of life, and to be nourished by the Tree of Life that brings healing and wholeness. Once we experience the spiritual deluge, it is essential that we sustain it by remaining in God's presence. This is where we must intentionally guard our hearts and prioritize our spiritual health. Just as a garden requires regular watering, pruning, and care, so too does our spiritual life. Here are some ways we can remain in a state of spiritual abundance:

- **Daily Connection with God**: Make time for daily prayer, worship, and Bible study. These spiritual practices keep us rooted in God and allow His living water to flow freely through us.

- **Guarding Against Distractions**: Just as a garden can be overtaken by weeds, our spiritual lives can be choked out by distractions. Stay focused on God's Word and keep your heart fixed on Him.

- **Embracing God's Rest**: Take time to rest in God's presence, allowing Him to refresh and replenish you. His Spirit is our ultimate source of strength and renewal.

- **Living in Community**: Surround yourself with other believers who can encourage you, pray with you, and help you stay grounded in God's truth. Community is essential for spiritual growth and sustainability.

Spiritual growth and renewal require intentional effort and focus. It's important to understand that spiritual transformation doesn't happen passively. We must take action to align ourselves with God's will, open ourselves to His presence, and continually nurture our relationship with Him. The purpose of this exercise is to help you identify practical steps that can lead you from spiritual dryness to spiritual deluge, from a place of parchedness to one of abundance, refreshing, and renewal. The journey involves recognizing where you are, identifying where you want to go, and taking the necessary steps to experience the fullness of God's presence in your life.

Practical Application: Moving Toward Spiritual Deluge

Spiritual growth and renewal require intentional effort and focus. It's important to understand that spiritual transformation doesn't happen passively. We must take action to align ourselves with God's will, open ourselves to His presence, and continually nurture our relationship with Him.

The purpose of this exercise is to help you identify practical steps that can lead you from spiritual dryness to spiritual deluge, from a place of parchedness to one of abundance, refreshing, and renewal. The journey involves recognizing where you are, identifying where you want to go, and taking the necessary steps to experience the fullness of God's presence in your life.

Here are some actionable steps to help you transition into a state of spiritual deluge:

1. Identify Your Desired Outcome

To begin, it is vital to understand what spiritual renewal looks like for you. This exercise invites you to reflect on your vision of spiritual deluge: what would it look like for you to experience a refreshing overflow of God's presence? What does your life look like when you are walking in God's abundance, peace, and joy? Spend time visualizing the desired outcome of this transformation and note any feelings or images that arise. This will give you a clear direction and serve as motivation as you begin the process of restoration.

Ask yourself:

- How do I feel when I am connected to God's presence?
- What aspects of my life change when I'm spiritually refreshed?
- What specific fruits do I expect to see in my spiritual life (e.g., peace, joy, confidence, intimacy with God)?

By clearly defining the desired outcome, you create a sense of purpose and vision for your journey to spiritual deluge.

2. Acknowledge Your Resources and Past Strengths

As you journey toward spiritual renewal, it's essential to reflect on the resources and strengths that have supported you in the past. These can include personal experiences where you've felt spiritually revived, powerful scriptures that have ministered to you, or spiritual practices that have helped you stay connected to God.

Reflect on how God has carried you through tough seasons before, and remind yourself that the same God who helped you then is with you now. To do this, ask yourself:

- What spiritual practices (such as prayer, worship, Bible reading) have been a source of strength in the past?

- When was a time I experienced deep spiritual connection or refreshing?

- How have I overcome previous periods of dryness?

By identifying these resources, you empower yourself to draw on them in your current season and build on past victories. Trust that the same tools that worked for you in the past will continue to sustain you as you press forward.

3. Set Small, Achievable Steps

The journey toward spiritual deluge requires consistent action, and the key to sustainable transformation is taking small, achievable steps. It is important not to overwhelm yourself with big expectations but to focus on practical, day-to-day actions that will lead you closer to your goal of spiritual restoration.

These small steps might include:

- Setting aside a specific time each day for prayer or Bible study

- Choosing a scripture to meditate on each week

- Attending a community group or Bible study for spiritual support

- Making space in your schedule for quiet time with God, where you can just be in His presence.

Starting with manageable, daily practices builds momentum and creates consistency, which is essential for lasting transformation. Over time, these small actions will compound, leading you to the abundant, overflowing life God has promised.

4. Recognize and Celebrate Moments of Spiritual Connection

As you work toward experiencing a spiritual deluge, it's important to take note of moments where you feel a sense of spiritual connection, even if they are small. These moments, however fleeting, are signs that God is working in your life. Celebrate these times of renewal as markers of progress, and use them as encouragement to keep moving forward. For example, you may feel refreshed after a time of prayer, or you may experience peace while meditating on a verse of Scripture. Take time to reflect on these moments and thank God for His presence.

Ask yourself:

- When did I feel a spark of spiritual connection or renewal this week?

- How did I respond to God's presence in that moment?

- What has changed in my heart, my mind, or my actions during those moments of connection?

Acknowledging these moments will keep you encouraged and remind you that the journey is worth it, even when the process feels slow.

5. Stay Committed to Daily Spiritual Practices

Maintaining a close connection with God requires intentional, daily effort. Just as a garden requires regular watering to stay vibrant, our spiritual lives require regular nourishment. Make spiritual practices a priority in your daily routine. These practices can include:

- **Prayer**: Make prayer a part of your daily life. Whether it's formal time set aside for deep prayer or short, spontaneous prayers throughout the day, remain in constant communication with God.

- **Worship**: Worship isn't confined to a Sunday service; it's a lifestyle. Worship God through music, through acts of service, or simply by reflecting on His goodness and grace.

- **Scripture Reading**: Dive deep into God's Word regularly. Use it for direction, encouragement, and wisdom. Scripture is alive and active, and it has the power to renew your spirit.

- **Silence and Solitude**: Carve out time to sit in the quietness of God's presence. Silence allows you to hear His voice clearly and to be replenished by His peace.

By staying committed to these spiritual practices, you keep yourself rooted in God's presence, which leads to sustained spiritual renewal.

6. Guard Against Spiritual Distractions

Distractions are one of the most common threats to spiritual growth. In the same way, a garden can become overrun by weeds; our spiritual lives can be choked by distractions, whether they are the busyness of life, unhealthy relationships, or emotional burdens. To sustain spiritual growth, it's important to guard against distractions and protect your spiritual life by:

- Setting boundaries with your time and energy

- Letting go of things that distract you from your spiritual health

- Prioritizing spiritual practices and relationships that nourish you

The more intentional you are about protecting your spiritual space, the more room you will have for the abundant life God wants to pour into you.

7. Embrace the Rest and Peace of God

As you journey into spiritual deluge, remember that God calls us into rest. It's not a race nor a burden, it's an invitation to experience the peace and refreshment of His presence. The rest God offers isn't about doing nothing; it's about trusting Him fully and letting His peace flood your soul.

Embrace this peace by:

- Taking time to rest in God, knowing that He is in control

- Letting go of the need to perform or prove yourself

- Learning to trust God's timing and His work in your life

When you embrace God's rest, you open yourself up to deeper levels of spiritual renewal, allowing His peace to flow into the deepest parts of your heart.

These steps are designed to help you move from spiritual dryness to spiritual deluge, where God's presence overflows in every area of your life. By acknowledging where you are, envisioning where you want to be, and taking intentional steps forward, you can begin experiencing the refreshing that only God can provide. His promise is clear: when we seek Him with our whole hearts, we will find Him (Jeremiah 29:13), and we will experience the abundance of life He offers through His Spirit. As you commit to these practices, know that God is with you every step of the way, bringing renewal, refreshing, and restoration. Keep your eyes on Him, trust in His process, and allow His Spirit to work within you as He leads you into a life of spiritual deluge.

Conclusion

God has created an oasis for us, a place where we can live in His presence, where His river of life flows, and where we are nourished and refreshed. Through Jesus Christ, we have been given access to the Tree of Life, and we can live in the fullness of God's promises. We have the power to pick up the mat of sin, depression, anxiety, illness, or any adversity and walk in the freedom God has for us. We can prophesy to the winds, trusting that God will breathe life into every dry, broken place.

As we return to the oasis of Eden, we will experience the fullness of God's presence, a place of rest, abundance, and renewal. May we continually live as a well-watered garden, bearing fruit in every season and allowing the river of life to flow endlessly from within us.

5 Key Takeaways for Meditation

- *Spiritual dryness is temporary, and God desires to restore us.*
  "When the poor and needy seek water, and there is none, and their tongue is parched with thirst, I the Lord will answer them; I, the God of Israel, will not forsake them." (Isaiah 41:17) NIV

- *The Yellow Zone requires caution, seek God before frustration leads to separation.*
  "As the deer pants for streams of water, so my soul pants for you, O God. My soul thirsts for God, for the living God. When can I go and meet with God?" (Psalm 42:1-2) NIV

- *God promises to fill us with living water in times of dryness.*
  "Jesus answered, 'Everyone who drinks this water will be thirsty again, but whoever drinks the water I give them will never thirst. Indeed, the water I give them will become in them a spring of water welling up to eternal life." (John 4:13-14) NIV

- *Transitioning from dryness to deluge requires repentance, seeking God's face, and returning to intimacy.*
  "If my people, who are called by my name, will humble themselves and pray and seek my face and turn from their wicked ways, then I will hear from heaven, and I will forgive their sin and will heal their land." (2 Chronicles 7:14) NIV

- *Sustaining spiritual health requires prayer, obedience, and community.*
  "Pray without ceasing." (1 Thessalonians 5:17) NIV
  "Rejoice in hope, be patient in tribulation, be constant in prayer." (Romans 12:12) NIV
  "And let us consider how to stir up one another to love and good works, not neglecting to meet together, as is the habit of some, but encouraging one another, and all the more as you see the Day drawing near." (Hebrews 10:24-) NIV

Personal Reflection Questions

1. What are the signs of spiritual dryness that I've noticed in my life?

2. How can I intentionally move from the Yellow Zone into a time of refreshing?

3. In what areas of my life do I need to experience a spiritual deluge?

4. How can I maintain sustainability in my spiritual walk after experiencing renewal?

Closing Prayer

Father, I acknowledge my need for You in this season. If I have drifted into a place of dryness, I ask for Your mercy to restore me. I desire to be filled with Your living water, to experience the deluge of Your presence. Refresh my soul, renew my strength, and help me to stay rooted in Your love. In Jesus' name, Amen.

Prophetic Release and Word of Encouragement

I speak over you today that God is bringing you from a place of dryness into an outpouring of His love and grace. You are entering into a time of spiritual renewal, where His presence will fill every part of you. Trust that the deluge is coming, and in it, you will find healing, restoration, and strength for the journey ahead.

CHAPTER 2

HE CALLED ME WORTHY: RISING THROUGH THE SHADOWS INTO PURPOSE

WRITTEN BY LA'TOYA GUILLORY

As a child, we went to church on the major holidays. I didn't have a relationship with God then, but I always felt He had his hand on my life. It wasn't until I was about ten years old that I realized that I had a purpose and that he was preparing me for something. I remember constantly feeling protected by Him, even in the darkest times of my life. At the same time, I felt the spirit of God telling me that I would help other people find their purpose. Regardless of what my life looked like at the time or where I was headed in life, He would use me to help others understand their worth. Now, at ten years old, not knowing who He was personally, I had no idea what I was walking into. I had no idea what helping others understand their value looked like, without first understanding mine. So, He took me on a journey to find myself. It took me years and decades to truly understand the woman He created me to be. There were many moments of self-doubt, depression, and childhood trauma that I had to walk through to understand my truth.

Each of us holds a unique story, a set of beliefs, and core values that shape who we are. Yet, in a world where expectations, roles, and comparisons constantly surround us, it's easy to lose sight of our worth and to waver in our confidence. Owning your truth, understanding who you are at your core, and embracing it without apology is foundational to living a life of true purpose. When we align with our truth, we unlock a deeper sense of value, one that isn't tied to anyone else's opinions, roles, or standards.

This chapter is about reconnecting with that unshakeable truth within yourself. It's about identifying and appreciating who you are regardless of your accomplishments, degrees, and job status. It's about using that awareness to fuel a life of genuine purpose. Living with purpose doesn't just mean setting big goals; it means being intentional about who you are, what you stand for, and the impact you wish to have on those around you.

Purpose creates direction, and with direction, we can walk through life confidently, no longer weighed down by doubts or by the need to seek approval. True confidence doesn't come from "feeling good all the time" but from an understanding that you are enough, just as you are. When you know your worth and walk in your purpose, and confidence naturally follows, not as an act, but as a way of being. This chapter will guide you through stories within scripture that will help uncover your truth, affirm your value, and build a purposeful life rooted in authenticity with God as your guide. By the end, you'll feel more empowered to take bold steps forward, with a confidence that grows from knowing, fully and deeply, who you are. Are you ready to walk in your truth, embrace your purpose, and live boldly? Let's dive in.

Own your Truth

Living intentionally starts with embracing who you are at your core. When we own our truth, we acknowledge our beliefs, values, and passions without fear of judgment or rejection. It's about being authentic and true to yourself in every aspect of your life.

Oftentimes we find ourselves going about life doing what's necessary to keep the train moving. We do our best to make sure the kids have what they need, our spouses are happy, and are sure to put our best foot forward at our nine-to-five. In the midst of all of this, life is happening.

Our kids are getting older, our parents are getting sick or passing away, and God knows what else. Life may be lifeing, but we can't stop now, right? So we push our emotions down and put on the emotions of everyone else.

Naomi found herself in the same situation. Naomi followed her husband and children to a foreign land due to a famine. Not long after, her husband dies and leaves her to care for their two sons. It is my belief that Naomi didn't truly give herself enough time to grieve because she had to pick up the pieces. Here she is in a foreign land with no family or friends to help her out. Naomi has no time to grieve, so she does what she has to do. She keeps moving. Not long after her husband's death, her two sons marry women from the land they now reside. While happy about the two new additions to the family, I imagine that Naomi probably had no idea how she was going to add them to the mix. Just as she begins to see some sort of normalcy, death claims her two sons. Naomi now has no husband, no sons, and no family. What she does have is purpose. The problem is she can't see it right now. She hasn't allowed herself to grieve what was and see what is.

Naomi hasn't learned to own her truth. The truth is Naomi was exhausted, she felt alone, she was lost. She knew how to be a wife and a mother, but all of that was taken away at least, she thought so. After trying to send her daughter-in-law back home to their families the relentless Ruth refused to leave her mother-in-law's side. Ruth gave Naomi her purpose back. I believe that she was God's love for Naomi in human form. Not only did she gain a daughter, but she gained her full inheritance in the land that God promised her and her family for generations to come.

Owning your truth begins by discovering your core values. We must take time to reflect on moments in our lives when we felt most fulfilled and at peace and identify the values that were present in those moments. Write them down and see if they align with where you are.

While Naomi understood her values of being a mother. I believe she didn't have the opportunity to gauge who she was as a woman. Her identity became lost due to feelings of having to do everything now on her own. I'm sure that her sons and daughter in laws pitched in where they could, but I have a feeling that Naomi was the type of woman that did not like to ask for help.

Owning your truth requires vulnerability. It means being open about your struggles, dreams, and fears. It means we must let people into those secret places that we are not ready to deal with. Here's the truth, not dealing with our authentic feelings towards whatever is going on in our lives does not make it less real. Embracing the truth does not mean that you will get over it faster, but it will help you deal with your raw emotions and help you heal before God takes you to that next place.

Once Naomi got to a place where she was able to acknowledge her truth, she began to see her strengths and understand her weaknesses. She realized that she still had breath in her lungs so that meant that she still had work to do. She may not have had her sons and her husband anymore, but she had Ruth. Ruth was so instrumental in helping Naomi see her true identity. Not the one that man gave her or that she gave herself, but the identity that was purposed for her by God. When we really take a good look at ourselves in the mirror and see ourselves the way that God intended us to. He will begin to show you who you are and what He has purposed for you to do.

Father,
We are tired, and we ask for your strength. You said that you would be everything we needed you to be in every moment because you are the I Am. Lord, we ask you to show us ourselves and remove everything that is not like you. We invite you to give us rest and help us to own our truth. Teach us to set emotional boundaries and heal us from all childhood and adult trauma. Transform us from the inside out in Jesus' name Amen

You Have an Assignment

David understood from an early age that he had an assignment. From tending sheep to slaying giants, regardless of the assignment, he was determined to follow through. No matter what ridicule he faced, from his outward appearance to the unexpected turn of events with Saul. He knew how to set emotional boundaries, cry out to the Father, and finish the race.

Everyone has a unique purpose. Your assignment in life is reflected by your passions, skills, and the problems you are passionate about solving. David was known as the man after God's own heart. The one thing that he was passionate about was pleasing God. He made sure that everything he did was done with excellence and honored God. If you are not familiar with the story, David was the smallest of all of Jesse's sons. He was sent out to the pastures as the sheep herder for his family. Though he was small in stature, he was mighty in God. To protect the sheep, he had to fight off lions, bears, and all other intruders who tried to come against his family's livestock. David was on assignment. Though his father and brothers did not have the best intentions for placing David in the field. God knew exactly where he was supposed to be.

I'm sure David wasn't thrilled about his assignment at first, but he knew that he had to do the best that he could with what he had, and God would do the rest. Once David overcame his emotions concerning his assignment, I believe he began to be intentional about what he was called to do. On a mission to please God, he began setting goals and becoming strategic about how he was going to protect their sheep. I believe he began to train himself how to fight off bears and kill lions. He knew that he had to be wise about what he was being called to do.

As we continue to walk into our purpose, I want to encourage you to do the same. With your purpose in mind, set goals that align with your assignment. Be SMART (Specific, Measurable, Achievable, Relevant, Time-bound) and create a clear action plan. Break down your goals into manageable steps to stay focused and motivated. Remember that the call is bigger than the circumstances that come with it. David understood that fighting off lions and bears came with his position, and he would not be moved.

As David got comfortable in his role, God decided it was time to call him higher. Little did he know that all the skills he learned in the field would be used for God's glory. One day David's father asked him to bring his brother's lunch to help them fight the army of the Philistines. As he approached the army, he realized that the army was backing down from a giant that had the nerve to talk about his God. David wasn't having it. Not only did he understand who he was, but he understood Who's he was. The army troops allowed fear and doubt to come into their camp and hinder their assignment. David, who was small in stature, was in the right place at the right time. How dare this uncircumcised Philistine talk about his God. With one slingshot and two smooth stones. David kills the giant and cuts off his head. What David didn't know was that God was preparing him to be King. All God needed was David's yes, and he would do the rest.

Doubt and fear can hinder your progress. When we begin to feel these emotions, we must explore strategies to overcome them. You can do this by reciting positive affirmations, creating visualizations like vision boards, and seeking support from mentors or friends who believe in your vision.

Slaying giants was only part of his assignment. As David began to make a name for himself, King Saul grew jealous of him and set out to kill him. David was loved by everyone, including the king's son, Johnathan. Unbeknownst to Saul, Johnathan made a covenant with David and gained favor in his sight. Saul tried everything in his power to destroy David, but his tactics were no match for God.

Saul began to understand that due to his disobedience, David would take his rightful place as king. This made Saul even more angry. He made it his mission to find David and kill him. The beautiful thing about this story is that no matter how far he had to run, how many hiding places he had to find, and how persistent Saul was to have him killed. David understood his assignment. David knew that he was more than capable of killing Saul, but that was not his purpose. His purpose was to honor God and do everything with excellence. As we continue this journey of life, remember that staying committed to your assignment requires discipline and perseverance. We must develop habits and routines that reinforce our goals and celebrate the small victories along the way.

Father,
Help us to stay focused on you. We ask that you show us how to persevere through the adversity that comes our way. Help us to always seek your ways and your guidance. We thank you that you've already gone before us. We come against all fear and doubt that would hinder us from going to that next place. We know that this assignment is bigger than us, and we surrender it to you now In Jesus' Name, Amen

Your Value Unveiled

Understanding your value starts with recognizing that you are inherently valuable, just as you are. We must reflect on experiences and messages that have shaped our self-worth, challenge any beliefs that undermine our value, and replace them with empowering truths. For some of us this may be hard to do. Finding value when you never felt valued is difficult. If you've listened to my podcast or follow my blogs, you may have heard me say this before. If so, it's okay the truth never gets old. If you find yourself in a place where you feel like you don't matter. I want to challenge you to consider this. The Bible tells us in Psalm 139:13-14 and again in Jeremiah 1:5 (NIV) that He knew us before we were in our mother's womb. Meaning, He had a purpose and a plan for us before we were even born. He was very intentional with making each and every one of us. He wanted us to experience life on this earth with Him in our hearts.

I'm so thankful that he has commanded my body to take in the right amount of air to make my heartbeat. I am grateful that the blood he has flowing through my veins flows to the appropriate places so my body can function the way that it needs to, and I am especially thankful that he gives me enough oxygen in my body to help it get the right amount of sleep so that I don't suffocate. My point is that while people on this earth may not have valued you, God does, and He shows us time and time again when He allows us to wake up in the morning. Just in case you need another example. Let's talk about the prodigal son.

The prodigal son was unsatisfied with his life and wanted to live on his own terms. His family was wealthy, so he knew that he had an inheritance, and requested it all from his father. While on his own, he began to live a life that was contrary to who he was created to be. He forgot who he was and Who he belonged to. He squandered all of his money and found himself eating with the pigs. After he humbled himself he decided it was time to go back home. What he didn't know was that his father would greet him with open arms. Something else that he didn't expect is that he would be met with sibling rivalry as well. His brother felt that the he shouldn't be honored because he was disobedient and left him behind to clean up his mess. Regardless of how his brother felt, the prodigal son gained assurance and understood that his value was worth more than anyone else's opinions.

The prodigal son learned a valuable lesson. He learned that his worth was not tied up in his money or lack thereof. Upon returning home, his father requested that the best robe be placed on him, he be given sandals for his feet and a ring on his hand. He was also given a fatted calf to eat. This was one of the highest honors that was given to him. Despite all the things he put his father through, he didn't reject him. He made sure that he knew that he was loved. Self-love is crucial for living intentionally. As much as we show compassion for others, we have to have compassion for ourselves as well. Treat yourself with the kindness you deserve and engage in activities that nurture your mind, body, and spirit, reinforcing your sense of worth.

Whether you want to believe it or not, you matter. Take time to celebrate your achievements, big or small and acknowledge your progress and the unique contributions you bring to the world. I know this is going to be easier said than done. I would encourage you to take inventory of who you allow in your inner circle.

Do these people uplift you or keep you down? Do they inspire you, or do they deplete you? If you are constantly trying to protect your peace when they are in your presence, they probably shouldn't be. Surround yourself with people who uplift and support your journey. Identify relationships that enhance your sense of worth and seek out communities where you can share your truth and grow together.

Father,

You call me worthy. I am so thankful for this life that you have given me. I will admit that sometimes it is hard to walk this thing out, but I know my worth and my value are in you. Father, I pray that you will protect my peace and help me identify people who should not be in my inner circle. I ask that you provide a strong support system for me to help remind me of my worth on those hard days. Give me the strength to be vulnerable to those who will help me grow and walk towards your vision for my life. In Jesus name, I pray, Amen.

Kingdom Confidence

Kingdom confidence is rooted in the understanding of your identity in a larger context. It helps you reflect on your beliefs and values and how they shape your confidence. Kingdom confidence reinforces your identity and purpose in a way that transcends self-doubt and gives you the strength to stand through adversity for such a time as this. Queen Esther is a good example of this. Queen Esther was put in a position that not many women were able to walk through. She was charged with putting her values and life on the line to save her people. The fate of her culture was in her hands despite laws regarding women's rights during that time. How did she get here?

After her beloved king just removed his previous wife for going against the laws that had been put in place. Esther was summoned to be next in line for her role. Esther, an orphan raised by her cousin Mordecai, was brought up understanding her worth and the value of loving people where they are. Esther was not the only virgin in the castle who was chosen to apply for that role, but she gained favor everywhere she went. Ultimately, Esther became the King's chosen wife. With confidence in her identity, Esther was able to embrace her kingdom assignment. She lived boldly, knowing that she was equipped and called to make a difference. Esther integrated her faith, values, and purpose into her daily life, inspiring others to do the same.

News came that the Jews would be destroyed, and it was up to her to save them. Esther was left with one question, how do you honor your husband and stay true to the assignment and core values that God gave you. Esther could not reveal her identity yet; she had to be strategic. She knew that Haman was the one behind the destruction of her family line. She also knew that if she didn't step up, her family lineage will be destroyed. With the confidence of God, she defied all rules and went into the king's court without being summoned. Esther was ready to put her life on the line by any means necessary. But God! God granted Esther favor as she pushed through the fear.

Her boldness unveiled the wickedness of Haman and the plots that he had to destroy her family. Her Kingdom confidence afforded her and her family the inheritance that they were promised for generations. Her kingdom's confidence reminded her of her kingdom's authority. God prepared her for that very moment. Now don't get kingdom confidence confused with pride or arrogance. There is a big difference. Though Esther understood that she had favor, she remained humble and trusted that God would guide her along the way. She aligned her perspective with God's and trusted the process.

Father,

Thank you for every door you allow me to walk through. I ask that you give me the Kingdom Confidence I need to walk through every door like I belong there. I ask, Father that you destroy all fear in me to do what you have called me to do. Father, your word tells us in Proverbs 18:16 that our gifts will make room for us and put us in front of great men. I ask that you close any door that is not from you. May your continued unmerited favor follow me all the days of my life. In Jesus' name Amen.

CHAPTER 3

DIVINE PURPOSE IS OUR MAKEUP

WRITTEN BY SHELIA HARRIS

Divine Purpose is about sharing your story with those who may not be inclined to listen but whose lives are forever changed when they do. It shapes our identity and reflects God's plan and intention for our lives.

Purpose is defined as the reason for which something is done, created, or exists. When I think about purpose, I don't see it as a singular, monumental aspect of life. Instead, I believe that purpose can be found in every part of our lives. This leads me to believe that purpose is the fabric of our existence. No matter what challenges you face or experiences you go through, there is always a purpose behind it.

Take a moment to reflect on your life, considering all the trials and triumphs you've encountered. Somewhere along the way, there has been a purpose for everything. In this chapter, you will discover how God has a purpose for you in your everyday life, whether it relates to your business, job, parenting, marriage, ministry, or, most importantly, within yourself. Yes, God has a unique purpose for you. Additionally, this chapter will reveal that your purpose may not look like what you initially expected.

Hello there! I'm excited to meet you! My name is Shelia Harris, and at 48, I cherish my role as a wife and mother to five wonderful children and four grandchildren. I'm excited to connect with you as your PURPOSE COACH, guiding you toward discovering your DIVINE PURPOSE. Through my own journey, I've received insights from GOD that I can't wait to share with you, and I hope that by the end of this chapter, you'll gain a deeper understanding of your own unique purpose!

What is Divine Purpose

So, what exactly is DIVINE PURPOSE? It's GOD'S beautiful plan and intention for our lives, shaping our futures and destinies. PURPOSE is the reason behind everything we do, create, and experience. It's comforting to know that God has thoughtfully counted our days and even the hairs on our heads, ensuring that every purpose He has for us will be fulfilled. Psalms 57:2 (NKJV), beautifully states, "I will cry out to God Most High, To God who performs (Purpose) all things for me." Just think about that for a moment!

I've realized that purpose isn't just one big achievement in life. It's a part of every single experience we have. From the tiniest moments to the grandest milestones, each has its own significance. I remember a day when I prayed earnestly for clarity about my divine purpose. I expected a single, definitive answer, but what I heard was enlightening, GOD revealed that my purpose lies in fulfilling His will, and this purpose unfolds throughout my life.

At first, I thought there was one grand vision I was meant to accomplish, but GOD reassured me there is so much more! He showed me that DIVINE PURPOSE resembles a pyramid with countless extensions. I found this to be exciting! It helped me visualize how our purpose branches out into various aspects of our lives. There's purpose in our families, marriages, children, careers, ministries, and even in our trials and tribulations.

Every challenge we face has a purpose too! As we journey together, I look forward to helping you uncover the layers of your own divine purpose, celebrating all the beautiful extensions that shape your life. Let's go on this journey together, your purpose awaits!

As I reflect on my journey, it's evident that all these experiences tie back to one central theme: PEOPLE. Our divine purpose is intricately linked to our interactions with others. Whether joyful or challenging, each moment in life serves a higher purpose, a divine thread weaving through our existence.

When I first embraced my faith at 18, I was often told to find my purpose. I imagined it would be deeply fulfilling, a passion that would light up my days without feeling like work. I thought it would be an exhilarating path. How many of you felt the same? Little did I know that my divine purpose would involve discomfort, humility, and a commitment to something greater than myself.

Looking back, I realize my initial understanding of purpose was limited. My journey has shown me that my passion fuels my purpose, but it is ultimately not about my desires but glorifying God and serving His people. Throughout my life, I've seen our purpose unfold in various ways, urging us to reach out and connect with others. Examining Jesus' life reveals the depth of His purpose on earth, a purpose centered around humanity.

Jesus understood he was born for a remarkable purpose, and the same goes for you! Your life is a beautiful design, not a coincidence or an error. Before your parents even dreamed of you, God envisioned a meaningful role for you. Just as Jesus was sent on a divine mission to offer His life for our salvation, you, too, have been crafted for something truly significant.

The Word of God reveals that everything, including our very existence, originates with Him. Uncovering your divine purpose requires nurturing a deep and personal relationship with God, as our true calling is found in Him. While our passions often resonate with our gifts and talents, it's important to remember that they don't solely define our divine purpose. Jesus had many extraordinary gifts, but His ultimate mission was to bridge the gap between God and humanity, bringing hope for eternal life. He served by feeding the hungry, healing the sick, raising the dead, and spreading the gospel, all vital pieces of His divine purpose to save the lost.

Just like Jesus' journey was centered on serving God's people in various ways, I'm eager to share my own journey of discovering purpose and the passions and talents that have beautifully shaped my path. Remember, there's a divine purpose within YOU waiting to be embraced!

Finish What You Started in Me, GOD…

What if your purpose was not what you expected?

Each one of us is blessed with a unique purpose, just as God and Jesus embodied their own incredible missions. The journey, however, often involves navigating our understanding of that purpose, or sometimes our misunderstandings. When we get a hint of what it might be, many of us excitedly rush to chase our individual visions, sometimes forgetting to invite the Father into our plans. It's important to remember that God's purpose for us could differ from what we initially envisioned.

We often view our purpose as a personal quest when, in truth, it's about God working through us to create a positive impact in the lives of others. Our aim should be to open ourselves up as vessels for God, allowing Him to fulfill His divine plan and reach those who really need His love and support, especially those who might feel overlooked or unworthy. It's a privilege to be woven into the beautiful tapestry of God's plan that spans generations.

Reflecting on my own journey, I remember feeling lost as a young girl, searching for the meaning of life. There were days when I felt hopeless, even wishing I wouldn't wake up, but God gifted me with another opportunity each morning, and sometimes that felt frustrating. The pain of harsh words from my dad and relentless bullying at school weighed heavily on my heart. I often felt unworthy as those hurtful comments echoed in my mind. My understanding of God then was limited to desperate pleas for relief, without grasping why I had to endure these challenges.

I'll always remember one particularly tough morning, around 15 or 16 years old, standing in front of the mirror with tears rolling down my cheeks. I was frustrated, belittling myself while focusing on every little flaw and comparing myself to others, feeling like I could never measure up. I didn't realize then that I was caught in a deceptive cycle while my life was meant for a much greater story.

At 17, everything changed. I felt drawn to read the Bible for reasons that were still unfolding. My initial search for comfort blossomed into an incredible journey of discovery. The more I engaged in the scripture, especially the New Testament, the more my perspective shifted. I even remember talking to my dad about cutting down the unfruitful peach tree in his friend's yard after reading one day!

Slowly but surely, I noticed beauty in the reflection that stared back at me. I would hear God whispering words of affirmation to my heart, restoring my confidence bit by bit. I reached a point where I could embrace the very traits I had once been bullied for. Even when I was unaware of the transformation, God was actively reshaping my life. What a powerful reminder that each struggle can lead to incredible growth!

I once asked God why He didn't take me when I wished He would. He gently reminded me that I had a purpose here. Although I did not grasp it all at once, I would eventually understand. God wanted me to discover who He created me to be.

When I talk about "Makeup," I'm really referring to understanding my identity through God's loving eyes instead of the world's often confusing standards. The creation story in Genesis tells us that we were formed thoughtfully in God's mind long before the world around us existed. Everything He made is beautiful and good, including each one of us! We came into this world with intention and a specific purpose, even before our first breath. Just think about what Jeremiah 1:5 tells us:

"Before I formed you in the womb, I knew you; before you were born, I sanctified you." (NKJV)

It is important for us to realize that every word God speaks over our lives is filled with purpose? Everything about who we are holds significance. Though we might not always grasp it in the moment, the closer we draw to God, the more He begins to reveal incredible truths about ourselves that we might never have known were there! My own journey of seeking God led to amazing revelations about my purpose.

We must embrace the idea that divine purpose has always been a part of us; we just needed the understanding to recognize it. God's divine purpose for our lives ultimately brings glory to His beautiful creation.

Ephesians 1:11-12 (NKJV) reminds us of this, saying, "In Him also we have obtained an inheritance, being predestined according to the purpose of Him who works all things according to the counsel of His will."

Isn't it exciting to know that as believers, we are here for a reason? We're not merely existing; we've been chosen. We belong to God and have been handpicked for a divine purpose. The Bible beautifully declares that we are a chosen generation, a royal priesthood, a holy nation, and His treasured people (1 Peter 2:9 NKJV).

So, let's rejoice in this truth! Each of us carries a purpose, and as we discover our identity through God's eyes, we unlock the potential to impact the world around us in remarkable ways. Together, let's embrace the journey ahead with open hearts and eager spirits!

Divine Purpose in Business

It all began when I was very young. I have always loved the beauty of God's creation and enjoyed looking at different things. Growing up, I noticed how my mom kept lots of pictures that held memories of important people in her life. As I got older, I wanted to do the same. I truly believe that a photo can preserve memories for a lifetime, transporting you back to the exact moment it was taken and how you felt then.

Although I've never attended photography school, I picked up a camera one day, marking the start of a beautiful journey that I fell in love with. During gatherings, I would capture the beauty in every moment, snapping pictures of everything and everyone around me. It was important to me to document various events throughout my life, my children's lives, and my family's lives so we could reminisce in the years to come.

Never in a million years did I think I would find a divine purpose in photography, but it happened. Photography felt natural and enjoyable; I never saw it as work or as something difficult. How hard could it be to snap a picture behind the lens? It was easy, but God revealed something deeper to me.

I realized God intentionally guided me each time I picked up my camera. It wasn't just about becoming a great photographer but about fulfilling a purpose.

Let me take you back to my senior year at Robert E. Lee High in Baton Rouge, Louisiana, a time bursting with laughter and joy! My best friend and I at the time would often find ourselves sitting on the side of the building, sharing funny stories, giggling uncontrollably, and playfully critiquing the unique outfits of people walking by. We even loved imagining how our classmates would evolve over time!

One day, I brought a camera along, eager to capture those enjoyable moments with our graduating friends. That day was a treasure, and those photos remain dear to us. Looking through them now brings a mix of nostalgia and warmth, some friends may no longer be with us, while others still share in our lives, but the happiness we experienced together is unforgettable.

As life unfolded, my passion for photography blossomed! I began documenting every family gathering and adventure we had. Each click of the camera was a chance to freeze time, reminding myself of where we were, who I was with, and how I felt during those precious moments. From birthday celebrations to vacations, I found beauty in capturing everything, from the people to the delicious meals we enjoyed.

I wanted to create memories for my family and me, and it brought such joy to see their smiling faces in those pictures! I especially loved snapping photos of my kids when they were little, preserving those fleeting moments forever. I genuinely believe that every photograph tells a story and keeps us connected to the ones we love.

I would have been skeptical if someone had told me years ago that I would become a photographer. I always saw myself simply as a person who loves taking pictures, not as someone with a purpose behind the lens. However, my admiration for the beauty of God's creation has truly transformed my life. I never envisioned that I would be engaged in something so meaningful, but God has an incredible way of leading us to our true calling.

He gently reveals our purpose without overwhelming us. In fact, it feels like I experienced a revelation that caught me by surprise in the most beautiful way, I just didn't realize how much I would touch the lives of others through my work. Looking back, I see that God was preparing me all along. What began as a cherished hobby blossomed into a hearfelt passion, driving me straight into my purpose. He has allowed me to see others through His eyes, and the journey has been nothing short of amazing.

I've discovered that God uniquely uses me to uplift and empower individuals, building their self-esteem and confidence. It's all about helping them recognize their worth as He sees them. The connections I've formed with people who needed what I have within me have been divinely orchestrated. Photography isn't just about capturing images; it's about showcasing God's glory and reminding people of their value.

When God unveils your divine purpose, you quickly realize it transcends any single perspective. It's expansive and will stretch beyond what you initially thought was possible. He maximizes our gifts and abilities in ways we can't always foresee.

As it says in Colossians 3:23-24 (NKJV), "Whatever you do, work at it with all your heart, as working for the Lord, not for human masters. Since you know that you will receive an inheritance from the Lord as a reward, it is the Lord you are serving." Embracing this truth has filled me with excitement and gratitude. I look forward to the journey ahead, knowing that it's all part of a beautiful plan.

Divine Purpose at Work

Have you ever found yourself questioning your purpose at work? It's easy to think we're there for the paycheck or the title, but there's often a much deeper reason for our presence in a particular role. As a person of faith, you may recognize that your job is more than just a job; it's a unique assignment from God. It's about reaching someone and impacting their life in ways you may not even realize.

I can relate to this deeply. From the very beginning of my career, I felt a strong sense of divine purpose in my role. I knew it was more than just a means to earn a living; I was there to fulfill a specific mission. For nearly five wonderful years, I worked at a place where I was not only comfortable but genuinely happy, great pay, weekends off, unlimited PTO, and colleagues who felt like family.

One unforgettable moment came when I felt God urging me to stay true to my beliefs, reminding me that people needed to see that I stood firm in my faith. I embraced this message wholeheartedly and made it my mission to let my light shine brightly at work. I took every opportunity to discuss my faith and share about my Savior. It became clear that many around me were hesitant to speak up about their beliefs due to fear of the consequences. But with respect and bold confidence, I chose to share my faith, the impact was great.

As time went on, I found myself praying for my coworkers and lifting them up with words of encouragement. I discovered that one of my colleagues had turned away from Christ, seeking fulfillment in other paths. He confided in me about his journey and how he had once been filled with the Spirit but had drifted away after facing significant struggles. Little did I know, God had placed me in that job specifically to rekindle his faith and lead him back to Christ.

Just a week before I was to leave my job, exactly as God had foretold, I received a heartfelt phone call from him. He thanked me for consistently sharing Christ with him and expressed how much he missed his relationship with God. Hearing him say that my presence had played a role in his journey back was incredibly moving. That moment solidified my understanding that God will place you in a role for the sake of just one soul if that is His will.

I've learned that no matter the challenges or the lengths of time, our purpose can resonate with those around us, illuminating the path for them. We each have the ability to be the light wherever we are. As it says in Matthew 5:14-16 (NKJV), "You are the light of the world. A city that is set on a hill cannot be hidden..." Let's each strive to shine our light brightly, showcasing our good works and ultimately glorifying our Father in heaven.

So, remember, your workplace is not just a job; it's an opportunity to fulfill your unique purpose and inspire others along the way. Let your spirit shine!

] God's intentionality is truly remarkable! Every detail of creation showcases His incredible purpose. Just think about it: from the very moment He spoke the universe into existence, everything was infused with meaning. Even the unseen aspects of life carry significance.

So, why would we ever think that God would leave us adrift in this beautifully crafted world without a purpose of our own? Each of us is designed to fulfill a divine purpose here on Earth!

It's important not to settle for a narrow view of what your calling might be. Give God the space to reveal the fullness of your purpose. Understand that purpose involves wholeness; it's a journey, not just a destination. You might find that you've been walking in God's divine purpose all along, perhaps without even realizing it! Each unique experience, every twist and turn, adds up to the beautiful tapestry of your life and ultimately connects you with His intentions.

Remember, God has equipped you to reach out to those who are lost, struggling with faith, feeling overwhelmed, or in need of encouragement. You have the power to uplift the weary, guide the doubtful, and bring healing to the broken. Your purpose extends to helping those who need growth or support, offering forgiveness, or leading others to Christ. God wants to use you as a vessel to make a difference in the world in so many amazing ways!

So, embrace this exciting journey! Keep your heart open and watch how God unfolds your purpose. There's so much beauty waiting to be experienced, and you have a vital role in it all. Let your light shine bright, and trust that you're exactly where you're meant to be!

Divine Purpose in Parenting

We often refer to it as sacrificing, but what God truly intends is for us to embrace our divine purpose in life. Initially, it may feel like a burden, especially for a single mother like myself, raising five kids. It's no small feat, and I've encountered countless moments where it felt like I was giving up so much. But through this journey, I've realized that what I see as sacrifice is part of a much bigger picture that God is unveiling.

Being a single parent throughout the bulk of my kids' younger years has taught me invaluable lessons. I always knew my role as their mother was significant, but I had no idea just how deep God's plan was for me in their lives. Every day presented its own set of challenges, and there were times when I felt entirely overwhelmed, questioning if I was truly capable of this journey. It was during those fragile moments that I would turn to God, asking, "Why me?" and longing for guidance on how to navigate the complexities of single parenting a large family.

When the challenges felt unbearable, I'll admit, I found myself retreating to my closet just to cry, to voice my frustrations, and to seek some sort of relief. But here's where things happened: that problem never really disappeared. Instead, it would always find a way to resurface, leaving me in a cycle of anguish. Then, one day, I heard a gentle yet powerful voice from God reminding me of the truth in my situation.

That moment of clarity was life changing. I realized I had been viewing my children as burdens rather than the beautiful blessings they truly are. Instead of seeing them as obstacles, I began to recognize that they are my greatest investments, rich opportunities for growth and love. I shifted my perspective and understood that rather than stopping my life, they had essentially enriched it beyond measure.

In my prayer closet, I cried, and when I came out, something inside me had changed. I adopted a new mindset, a purpose-driven mindset. I committed to being the best mother I could be, pouring into each of my children spiritually, emotionally, mentally, and physically. I finally understood why God had entrusted me with their care; it was about reliance on Him, which strengthened my faith.

Now that my children are adults, looking back, I understand just how intentional God has been in my life. To be chosen as the mother of these five incredible individuals was an act of faith on His part. God believed I could fulfill this divine role and do the necessary work to guide them. He knew I would give my all, even when it felt overwhelming.

Yes, it might sometimes seem like we're sacrificing our lives for our children, but remember, this is an investment in a greater purpose. Each moment spent nurturing and guiding them is a beautiful part of God's Kingdom and His plan. I'm proud to tell my children that God is always glorified through our lives and that they, too, will one day share this legacy with their own children.

As Proverbs 22:6 beautifully reminds us, "Train up a child in the way he should go, and when he is old, he will not depart from it." This is not just a promise; it's a profound truth. My role as their mother has been driven by purpose, and I cherish the opportunity to impart that same understanding to them. Together, we are all part of a divine story crafted by God, with each of us playing a significant role in sharing His glory.

Divine Purpose in Marriage

When we think about marriage, focusing on ourselves and what we might gain from the relationship is easy. However, when we dive into what the Word of God tells us about marriage, we discover it's a beautiful journey that extends far beyond individual desires. I used to view marriage through a limited lens, somewhat to the fairytales on TV, believing it to be solely about my happiness and personal fulfillment. It took time for me to understand that God's vision for marriage is different from worldly portrayals.

God created marriage as a sacred covenant; it's a timeless institution that has existed since the very beginning. Within this sacred bond lies a divine purpose, one that is uniquely tailored for each couple. You might wonder, "How does my marriage fit into this grand purpose, and what is my role in it?" Let me share my insights with you!

When I spoke about purpose earlier, I mentioned that it's part of God's plan for each person's life, including their future and destiny. Interestingly, before you even dreamed of being married, God had already laid out a plan for that relationship. Even before you met your spouse, God knew you were destined for this partnership. He designed marriage for deep companionship (as illustrated in Genesis 2:18-24 NKJV), procreation (Genesis 1:28, NKJV), and to serve Him alongside your spouse, your children, and through your unique life journey. This, my friend, is your divine purpose in marriage.

Reflecting on my own first experience with marriage, I recognized that I stepped into it at around 20 years old, lacking comprehensive biblical knowledge about the institution. My understanding was limited to what I observed in my parents' marriage and what I thought society expected of me. I felt the pressure to marry to avoid sinful choices and was eager to comply with what I believed was God's directive that it's better to marry than to burn with passion. However, despite taking this significant step, my lack of understanding of my purpose within that marriage led to challenges, ultimately resulting in divorce.

Fast forward to the present, and I find myself enriched with knowledge about my divine purpose in both marriage and life. Today, navigating my current marriage feels far more fulfilling because I understand what biblical marriage is truly about, the principles God has set for it, and my purpose as a spouse through His eyes.

On my wedding day, I remember the quiet moments before I walked down the aisle, it was just me and God in the room. In that moment, I felt the weight of His words: "Your life is about to change. From this day forward, you will never walk as the single version of yourself again." He shared with me that old parts of my identity would die as I approached the altar, making way for a new chapter in my life. With a willing heart, I responded to God, "Let Your will be done; I'm ready for what you have in store for me."

But God's message didn't stop there. He asked me a powerful question that resonated deeply: "Will you vow to take care of the son I am giving you?" It struck me that we often put the focus on men being questioned and evaluated by fathers before committing, but here was God, gently reminding me of the significance of nurturing and caring for my partner, as He values him deeply too.

As my husband and I stood at the altar, we both recognized that we were shedding our old selves, transitioning from two singles into a unified partnership. Our commitment was to love, serve, uplift, support, and pray for one another without reservation. In that moment, we understood that we were not just partnered by chance; we were intentionally placed together for a purpose. I realized that I was designed for him, and he was destined to be my companion.

In my marriage, I now clearly see my divine purpose and the reasons God brought us together. Together, we are called to cover each other, be each other's encouragers, prayer warriors, and champions. We help one another grow, stand by each other in moments of weakness, believe in one another's potential, and speak life into each other's dreams. We are called to push each other forward into our divine assignments, and together, we break generational curses, forging a path toward fulfillment and divine destiny.

As you reflect on your own journey in marriage or preparation for it, remember that it's about so much more than just the individual. Embrace the beautiful purpose God has for you and your partner, and step into this life-changing journey with confidence, joy, and a heart full of love!

Purpose is an incredible journey with a clear beginning, middle, and end! Just like Joseph in Genesis 37-50, who started with dreams, navigated through the details, and ultimately saw his visions come to life, we too have our own unique path to uncover. The first step is discovering what your divine purpose is. It's true that many of us haven't found it yet, and even those who do may feel ready to give up in the challenging middle phase. But don't lose heart! Each obstacle is just a stepping stone on the way to realizing your dreams. Remember, purpose is about more than just you; it's about how you impact the world. So let's embrace every moment, push through the tough times, and stay optimistic, you never know how close you are to the beautiful manifestation of your purpose!

Divine Purpose in Ministry.

Discovering your divine purpose in ministry is truly an exciting journey! It's about embracing the unique calling that God has placed on your life, allowing you to serve others in a way that only you can. Each of us is part of the magnificent body of Christ, and while our gifts may occasionally overlap, God has designed each of our purposes to be distinct. This diversity is what enriches our community and helps us all grow together.

To be on this incredible path, we need to earnestly seek God's presence. Our primary focus should always be on pleasing Him by doing His will rather than our own. Imagine the joy of knowing that your ministry purpose involves loving and serving others, sharing the love of God, offering godly guidance, and helping people grow spiritually, mentally, and physically in the way God intends for them.

When you embrace your calling with intention, every action you take will lead others closer to Christ, that is the heart of ministry!

In II Corinthians 3:2-6 (NKJV), we find a beautiful reminder of who we are as believers. We are living letters, or "epistles," written in the hearts of those around us, reflecting the gospel of Christ. Our lives are a testament to God's transformative power, and through us, others can experience His love and grace.

Ministry is so much more than what many people might think. It's not about personal gain or popularity; it's about setting aside our own desires and fully committing to God's purpose. Our role is to shepherd God's flock, leading, teaching, and nurturing those He has placed in our care. It's vital to remember that each of us has a special purpose in this beautiful tapestry; no effort is too small, whether it's keeping the church clean or tending the grounds. Every act of service contributes to God's mission.

I have a vivid memory of attending a church where I had the privilege to learn for three years. One Sunday, they held a special ordination service for new ministers. My pastor and his wife, with their own pastor by their side, guided those being ordained through a heartfelt commitment to God. They posed questions: "Are you ready to die to self and embrace the purpose God has for you? Do you comprehend that it's no longer about you, but all about God?" That day was pivotal for me, as I truly grasped the sacrifices that Jesus and His disciples made in the name of the Gospel.

Our ministry purpose is to reach the lost, embrace a servant's heart, and be willing to lay down our lives for the sake of the Gospel. It's easy to slip into a mindset where ministry becomes about personal gain, but as Jesus teaches us in Luke 9:23 (NKJV), true followers are called to deny themselves, take up their crosses daily, and follow Him. When we internalize this, we begin to understand our purpose in ministry and every aspect of our lives.

Additionally, Psalm 24:4 (NKJV) tells us that those with clean hands and pure hearts, who do not trust in idols or false gods, will receive blessings from the Lord. This passage reminds us that living a life aligned with God's values leads to profound blessings and vindication.

The journey to fulfilling your divine purpose in ministry is a remarkable adventure filled with growth, hope, and the incredible opportunity to touch lives. Embrace your unique calling wholeheartedly! Whether it's through singing, teaching, serving in the background, or providing emotional support, every role is vital to the body of Christ. Let's celebrate the diverse ways God works through us, and commit ourselves to serving with joy and enthusiasm. Together, we can make a lasting impact and draw many closer to His heart!

CHAPTER 4

Thriving Beyond Adversity

written by Jakeithia Prejean

Adversity has seemed to be a real thing these past few years. Navigating what was can seem difficult. There are times when we can't seem to get past the unfavorable times. You're not alone. Life brings adversity but just know you can get through it. There are times when adversity seems to be a constant thing. Adversity seems to find you even in times where you are already going through. There's a saying, "If it ain't one thing, it's another". Or maybe you've told yourself every time I take one step forward I take two steps back. These statements are very well true. Just know that adversity will come, but you can thrive through it. Thriving through adversity is imperative in order to live purposefully. The word thrive means to prosper or flourish. It means to be successful, perform, and develop in a successful way. John 16:33 says, "I have told you these things, so that in me you may have peace. In this world, you will have many trials and sorrows.. But take heart! I have overcome the world. " (NIV)

What are the things? The adversity, the sorrow, the disappointment, the grief, the pain, the heartache. We don't welcome these things but we do go THROUGH these things. The key here is to go through and not to stay stuck in survival mode. There are ways when we can thrive through adversity.

Letting go of the OLD.

In order to thrive beyond the adversity, we have to let go of the old. The old … can be hard to let go. Habits, patterns, and familiarity are often areas we tend to stay stuck in. We often stay in these places even when they no longer suit us. We're not happy, there is no joy, we feel like we're suffocating.

It could be your career, a town, friendships, or even relationships. One thing I know is that change can be scary, but it's inevitable. If we don't let go of the old and embrace the new, we will always be stuck and never grow.

Let's talk about letting go. Letting go means we relinquish the grip on something or even someone. Letting go of old ideas, old memories, old trauma and drama. We have to let go of old mindsets or what used to be. It's never an easy process. If we relinquish what's old we can embrace the new. It's time to let go of what was…let go of the thoughts of what you think should have been. We have to see change as a good thing. You can't keep looking back at the old, at what failed, at what didn't work. Letting go of the old allows room for what's best and what's better. The Bible says in Isaiah 43:18-19, (NIV)

"Forget the former things; do not dwell on the past. See, I am doing a new thing! Now it springs up; do you not perceive it? I am making a way in the wilderness and streams in the wasteland."

Ask yourself what do I need to let go? Are you willing to let go? God wants to make a way in the wilderness. The wilderness is the adversity, the hard thing, the past, the grief, the pain. He will make a way for the new; he will make a way for you if you're willing to let go of what was and make room to embrace what can be and what shall be. Streams can flow in the wasteland. The wasteland represents the place where it's been hard, the place that seems forsaken, the place where things have been dull and stale. God will bring streams that represent life, healing, prosperity, and success. He can remove the old and bring the new. Do you want it?

Learning to Intentionally Prioritize

After we let go of the old we have to be intentional about embracing the new. There are old things that no longer serve us. I want you to know that you can intentionally prioritize in order to thrive through adversity. To be intentional means to be deliberate, to be done on purpose.

I want you to take a moment and identify three areas in your life where you've faced adversity. What are they? Now, let's shift the focus. These aren't just pain points, they're power points. Let's be intentional about turning these areas into priorities. Why? Because where you once struggled is exactly where you're being called to rise and thrive.

The first thing you need to be intentional about is your faith. You must have faith in God. Have faith in knowing that he doesn't want you to stay in the place of adversity forever. He desires for you to come THROUGH the adversity more than you do. Faith shall arise in you, and faith to believe that God will do what he said in Isaiah 43:18-19. He can, and he will do it. Let's talk about how you can make your faith a priority. The Bible says faith comes by hearing and hearing by the word of God. Romans 4:17, (NIV). Before you have faith in God, you must know what God says about your situation. I admonish you to find scriptures that pertain to the adversity you're facing or have faced. What does God say about it? Read and meditate on it. Say what he says and believe what he says. You have to meditate on what he says; this will build your faith and trust in him.

I can tell you a thousand stories of how God makes promises that he keeps. His word is true, and his word is his promise. People have failed you, but God won't ever fail you. Make faith your priority. Another way to be intentional about your faith is to pray to word.

Every morning, I pray Psalm 91, which my grandmother taught me many years ago. There have been many times I've almost had an accident, but because God's word is true, I've been spared.

What areas do you desire to change, or what areas of your life have you faced adversity? One thing that I did a few years ago was to make my mental health a priority, along with my faith in God and going to therapy, I began to see a significant change in who I was to where I am now. We are made of three parts: mind, body, and spirit. Therapy helped me focus on my mental health. It helped me identify troubling thoughts and emotions from past hurts. It also helped me navigate adversities that were present at that time and helped me develop healthier habits. It helped me to address the root problems and explain how I feel so that I can thrive. It helped me transition from surviving to thriving.

What area do you need to prioritize in your life? How can you be intentional in prioritizing the things that matter? If you are feeling overwhelmed, choose three areas of your life that you need to intentionally prioritize. Many times, we tend to constantly neglect ourselves because of other obligations. You don't have to feel guilty about putting yourself first. Choose yourself today!

Remember, God wants you to be healthy and whole. He wants you to overcome adversity and help you do so. You must make a decision that you want to change, that you want something new.

_____
_____
_____
_____
_____
_____
_____
_____

Overcoming Adversity

There was a time when I had to overcome MUCH adversity. The beginning of 2021 started off with the biggest heartbreak of my life. I was hit with a very difficult issue. Not long after that, a dear friend of mine passed away, and another friend stopped talking to me for a reason I wasn't sure of. While I was trying to navigate the biggest heartbreak of my life, another friend moved away, one of my students was murdered by a former student, I got Covid, and then I experienced another person dying, all while trying to navigate a new way of life. I went to work as an educator with the fear of possibly having Covid again or my students having it. We had to navigate virtual learning and not being able to be close to loved ones cause of the possible infection of this disease. On December 1, 2021, I decided that I would no longer live and carry the weight of that year. I had been in weekly therapy for months, constant prayer, fasting, and changing. I made a decision that this adversity would not plague me any longer. One way to overcome adversity is to make a decision to do something about it. It was time for me to thrive, and I decided to live in that truth. You see, decisions are life-changing and powerful. All year I had made little decisions like forgiveness, processing grief, embracing change, and changing my perspective. It was at that moment I realized all those subtle processes changed me for the better. Adversity changes us. How we respond to that change is what matters.

In order to overcome adversity, I had to take accountability for how I responded. Some things we can't control but taking responsibility for our role in adversity will allow us to begin to make the change that is needed. In order to be liable, we must be humble and honest with ourselves. What can we do better now? What can we change now? Be intentional and prioritize by making the change. What lesson did we learn? Are you repeating the same mistakes? What old patterns and habits do we need to break?

One way I took accountability for my own adversity was I realized I never dealt with trauma and drama...I just tucked it and kept moving. It was like an ever-ticking bomb that could explode at any moment. I never gave myself the ability to grieve, to process things, or to sometimes even cry. I didn't deal with what bothered me instead, I ran from the pain, the hurt, the disappointment. When I would pray, God would give me the grace to process it, but at times I would shut him out. I had to become accountable to myself for how I handled adversity.

Thriving in the NEW

In order to thrive in the new, you must embrace the new. You have to enjoy and realize that in order to grow and thrive you must become new. Do something different. I want you to thrive in the new and give yourself some grace. What do I mean? Give yourself some time to navigate through the new. It will be uncomfortable at first but that's ok. Give yourself some time to adjust. Make room for mistakes and learn to thrive in what's new. Take your time and live in the moment.

Thrive means to prosper or flourish, to grow and develop well. Are you ready to Thrive? I want to share a way that you can thrive in the NEW.

Rest......

REST, my friend, Do you have too many responsibilities? Are you taking on more than you can handle? Can you delegate some of those responsibilities to someone else? Can you get someone to help you?

What is resting? It's ceasing from work or movement to relax, refresh oneself, or recover strength. Do something you enjoy. What brings you peace or joy? For instance...I love the water. It relaxes me. If I can't go canoeing or kayaking, I will go and sit by a lake or the pool. It's so refreshing to me.

I'm a teacher and I hear chatter all day so being by the water is peaceful. It's quiet and it helps me relax. Resting is OK!! Resting is being human. It's not being selfish. Too many times we "grind and grind" without giving ourselves time to rest. It's good to take moments of rest or even set aside a day to rest. You will be more productive if you aren't so tired. It's ok to work and rest. Some of us have this mentality if we don't do it, it won't get done. This pattern can come from being overly independent, never asking for help, always working, and never resting. We can't be our best selves when we're tired. Our body needs rest.

As an educator, Monday-Friday is a busy time for me because I'm teaching lesson planning, lesson adjusting, meetings, grading papers, etc. I'm intentional about resting on the weekends. Usually, I listen to my body and sleep in on a Saturday. This is because I need to be super intentional about giving myself proper REST. You might be saying I just can't seem to REST, there are too many things to do. Music helps me relax because I love to sing. I've been singing all my life. Music and singing are a happy place for me. Also, silence helps me relax; it has become therapeutic.

You can REST! Rest is a big part of resetting. For instance, some days, I do NOTHING!! Do you hear me? Not a thing. Maybe you can't do a whole day, but you can do an hour or two. I remember in college my best friend had a calendar of her day. She would schedule a time of rest and I would look at her crazy. It was only years later that I understood that REST is important. It is crucial to your success. You can't be as productive if you're always tired! GET SOME REST!!

At times you will need to REST and pause because you're drained and burned out. Sometimes this can happen in our career. Since I've been teaching in the school system for 18 years, I've experienced this. I remember a few years ago I took half of the semester off even though I love what I do. I was just tired, and I was questioning if teaching was something I needed to continue to do.

This is what I realized; that sometimes we quit things because we simply need to take a break or pause. I was thinking maybe teaching is just not for me anymore. I needed to pivot and embrace what no longer worked for me anymore. Education chose me, while I am no longer in the classroom, I find myself educating people in different ways. You can REST! Rest your mind, rest your heart! No fear, No worry and no anxiousness. Rest in what God said! What did he say? The bible tells you what he said. REST in his promises. Rest knowing that he's not a liar! Rest knowing that he will deliver you from adversity. Just REST.

Another way to thrive is to be your authentic self. Maybe you've heard it like this..." to thine own self be True." Never let people's actions or decisions change who you are. Be true to yourself. I hear this so much ...I match the energy. What does that mean? I'm more committed to being who I am. You can still be true to your character and create healthy boundaries for yourself. Don't just survive to thrive. I told this to my counselor once. I said I've been in survival mode, but I don't want to be like that anymore. I want to Thrive. I realized that self-preservation, self-sabotage, and fear were holding me back from thriving. I decided that I was going to be true to myself and deal with it. Too many times we go through life being comfortable or living comfortably. We can't thrive by barely getting by. We must grow and develop well.

The best project you can ever work on is You! You don't have "control" over everything. You can only do your part!! I live by this in regard to other people ..." I can't expect an apple tree to produce pears." What that means is that people are going to be who they are. We can't expect a rotten tree to produce any good fruit or fruit at all. In the RESET, we may find that people aren't who you think they are. It's a RESET of your perspective; you can't expect them to be something that they're not. We can't cut everyone off, but we can have healthy conversations and then, if need be, create healthy boundaries. We also must realize that some things are toxic. It could be your mindset, a person, your eating habits, etc.

Please understand that part. What I mean by that is sometimes the RESET may involve other people. You can't change anyone, but you can change how you respond. You can create boundaries, and you can say NO. In this RESET, there will be some things you will have to get rid of altogether. For instance, your mindset, or maybe that job because you're really an entrepreneur. Don't be afraid to be creative. You might not have seen your idea before, which is not a bad thing. Step out and do it!! When normalcy leaves, you have to find creative ways to get that thing done or to create new things. You have to decide that you want to thrive. Use some wisdom and use some faith too. This is a NEW path, and no one can tell you how to navigate through it but God.

The last thing to grow on a tree is its fruit; therefore, don't quit and keep going! You are valuable, don't let anyone tell you differently. Be humble but aware of your worth and what you bring to the table. Take time to enjoy the simple things in life. Work on you for you. It's your moment to thrive. We can't be afraid of the future; we have to prepare for it. Stop procrastinating; you're holding up your blessings. Just get it done. You may have "failed," but focus on what you have learned. Focus on the lesson. Never let anyone devalue who you are, including yourself. Never let anyone devalue your dreams, goals, and blessings. Don't just think about it; do it. Take steps toward thriving. Start somewhere. Take that first step, and the rest of the steps will be clear. Stay prayerful, and let God lead you.

What do you need to do to thrive in the NEW?
Write it down here and share it with a trusted friend. YOU got this!!

_____

_____

_____

_____

_____

_____

_____

_____

_____

_____

_____

_____

Reference: *Prejean, J.* (2022,2023). R.E.S.E.T.: Re-evaluate Everything So Everything Thrives. RESET Enterprises.

CHAPTER 5

Principles of Kingdom Economics

Written by Dr. Sharmonia Wimberly

Kingdom economics operates on principles vastly different from the world's systems. While earthly economics focuses on self-preservation, accumulation, and competition, God's economy is rooted in stewardship, generosity, and faith. Jesus taught this upside-down perspective, emphasizing that true riches come from a heart aligned with God's purposes. To live by Kingdom principles, believers must first understand that all wealth originates from God, our role is stewardship, and the divine law of sowing and reaping governs increase.

"In order to live financially free, you must begin by first pulling off all the baggage and excess layers of life to discover your true potential from within." Coach Mona

God's Ownership of Everything

The foundation of Kingdom economics begins with acknowledging God as the ultimate owner of all things. Psalm 24:1 (NIV) declares, *"The earth is the Lord's, and everything in it, the world, and all who live in it."* This verse sets the tone for how believers should view wealth: it's not ours. We are managers of God's resources.

The implications of God's ownership are transformative. If God owns everything, then everything we possess, our income, talents, time, and resources, has been entrusted to us for His purposes. Haggai 2:8 (NIV) reinforces this truth: *"The silver is mine, and the gold is mine,"* declares the Lord Almighty.

Practically, this mindset frees us from the burden of ownership. We no longer need to obsess over accumulating wealth or fear losing it, because we recognize that our role is not to hoard but to manage what God has given.

A modern-day example might be a business owner who dedicates a portion of their profits to funding missionary work or community development, recognizing that their success is ultimately God's.

I love this assurance that God gives us. Everything belongs to him. I started my business Shakyra Renee' Jewelry Collection with the concept of helping others become debt-free and financially stable. I offered business ownership to those who would like to start a small business with a small investment. The blueprint is designed to create profit sharing for individuals; as well as, a way to build their credit. I used affiliate marketing as a way to help others generate wealth for everyone. I chose to dedicate a portion of my profits back into the community. What are some ways you can show God you are a good manager of his resources?

Let's Pray:

Psalm 24 declares, "The earth is the Lord's, and the fulness thereof; the world, and they that dwell therein." Lord, I acknowledge your presence and humbly seek your wisdom in creating and building Kingdom Wealth. I immediately move forward with the confidence of financial wholeness. Therefore, I decree and declare wise money handling, genius creativity, manifesting wealth, and sound income producing investments. In Jesus' name Amen

Stewardship vs. Ownership

The concept of stewardship is central to Kingdom economics. Jesus emphasized this principle in the Parable of the Talents (Matthew 25:14-30 NIV). In the story, a master entrusts his servants with varying amounts of money, expecting them to invest and grow it while he is away. Upon his return, he rewards those who were faithful and condemns the one who buried his talent out of fear.

This parable teaches that God expects us to wisely manage whatever He places in our care, whether little or much. Stewardship involves intentionality, effort, and accountability. 1 Corinthians 4:2 (NIV) reminds us, *"Now it is required that those who have been given a trust must prove faithful."*

Faithful stewardship goes beyond finances, it extends to how we manage relationships, opportunities, and time. For instance, a Christian professional can steward their career by using their influence to mentor others, advocate for ethical practices, and create opportunities for Kingdom impact. We must be great stewards of what we have. We must challenge ourselves to maximize our finances while achieving your personal and business goals. Here are some basic and quick steps you can take are:

Personal Strategy:

1. Analyzing current bills and obligations.
2. Strategic plan and blueprint for bill pay disbursements
3. Reviewing the cost of credit and interest rates for reduction.
4. Identify money wasters and blockers.
5. Strategy for paying off debt

Business Strategy:

1. Analyze Business Revenues and Expenses
2. Analyze Business Bankability
3. Review Assets and Liabilities
4. Assist with Strategy for Business bookkeeping
5. Review Business Structure and Credit Worthiness

I have witnessed much success when clients incorporate these steps. I also include prayers and journaling to break generational and foundational patterns and cycles that hinder our finances. " How to Successfully move from stagnation, delay and setback to breakthroughs in finances."

The journey to our financial breakthroughs is evident in our obedience. Remember, patience is the virtue of this lesson and accountability is the skill. Command your success by holding yourself accountable. How do you hold yourself accountable? Hold yourself accountable by being committed to eliminating habits that cause personal and financial instability (i.e., poor credit, high interest rates, worry, no savings). While using the action plans, be "open" to creating "better".

Let's Pray: Thank you Heavenly Father for your guidance in streamlining my monthly expenses. Give me your financial wisdom and reveal the resources necessary to maintain stability during this time of reorganization. You said, "I the Lord search the heart, I try the reins, even to give every man according to his ways, and according to the fruit of his doings" (Jeremiah 17:10, KJV). God, I choose Your way of increase, and open my life up to new possibilities. Therefore, I decree and declare that I will obtain and maintain financial stability and prosperity!

Principles of Sowing and Reaping

One of the most profound laws in Kingdom economics is the principle of sowing and reaping. Galatians 6:7 warns, "Do not be deceived: God cannot be mocked. A man reaps what he sows." This principle applies to every area of life, including finances, relationships, and spiritual growth.

In the natural world, a farmer who sows seeds in fertile soil can expect a harvest. Similarly, when we sow generously into God's work, we position ourselves to receive blessings that go beyond material wealth. 2 Corinthians 9:6-8 affirms this: "Whoever sows sparingly will also reap sparingly, and whoever sows generously will also reap generously."

Sowing is not limited to tithing or giving in church. It includes acts of kindness, helping those in need, and investing time and resources into initiatives that advance God's kingdom. For example, supporting a struggling family, sponsoring a child's education, or volunteering at a local ministry are all forms of sowing that yield eternal rewards.

I can recall when I had rededicated my life to Christ. I belonged to this small Ministry. The Holy Spirit was definitely present in this ministry. I desire to follow God's word and to be obedient to every instruction in which he had given me. On one particular Sunday, God has spoken to me and told me to give a family friend my entire paycheck. I remember saying, "Really God, I need this money." I did not know that the family was in jeopardy of losing their home. Their home was in foreclosure. Out of obedience, I went to the young lady and gave her a check for the entire amount of my paycheck. It was approximately $1,200 at the time. The woman was so elated. She began to praise God and thanked me for the seed that I had given her. It wasn't until that time that I learned that her home was in foreclosure.

Years later, I saw the effect of my obedience and the seed that I sowed manifest in my life. I was going through financial hardship. I was struggling to keep my marriage while losing my home. And God showed me how my faith was put to work. How obedience brings a reward. I reminded God that he had given me my home. My property was in foreclosure for close to two and a half years. The judge had rewarded the bank back my home. I never gave up on my faith. I said God your word says seek ye first the kingdom of God and your righteousness and all things shall be added unto me. I also, reminded God of all the Seeds that I had sown. In less than 60 days, my attorney came back with a settlement. The bank discovered that they did not follow proper procedures when placing the foreclosure. Therefore, they reinstated my mortgage. Wrote off $250,000 worth of debt.

Lowered my interest rate to 2% and wrote off my equity line of credit of $100,000. I always think back to how important it was to be obedient to God's voice. Sowing and weeping is very important you never know when your Harvest will come. You never know how it will come but the word will never fail.

Let's Pray: Thank you Heavenly Father for your guidance in intentional giving and receiving. Keep my heart open to your voice of discernment. You said, "Give, and it shall be given unto you; good measure, pressed down, and shaken together, and running over, shall men give into your bosom. For with the same measure that ye meet withal it shall be measured to you again" (Luke 6:38 NIV). I decree and declare that every good gift prospers and operates in your definition of giving and receiving.

The Multiplication Principle

God's economy thrives on multiplication, not addition. In John 6:1-13 (NIV), Jesus demonstrates this principle when He feeds five thousand people with five loaves and two fish. After giving thanks, the small offering is multiplied to meet the needs of the multitude, with leftovers to spare. This miracle teaches that when we entrust what little we have to God, He can multiply it far beyond our expectations. It also encourages us to approach giving with faith rather than fear.

When I first started my small jewelry business, I barely had enough money to buy materials for a handful of pieces. It felt insignificant compared to the dreams I had in my heart. But instead of giving up, I dedicated what I had to God, asking Him to bless the work of my hands. Little by little, sales began to grow. One customer told a friend, then that friend told another. Opportunities came for pop-up shops and online sales I hadn't even planned for. What began as a few pieces on a small table multiplied into a thriving brand reaching people far beyond what I could have imagined. Just like the five loaves and two fish, God took what I offered in faith and multiplied it beyond my limited resources.

Let's Pray: Father, thank You for being the God of multiplication. We surrender what we have into Your hands, trusting that You can do more with it than we ever could on our own. Help us to give freely, believe boldly, and watch You move mightily. Increase our faith to see beyond what we have and into what You can do. In Jesus' name, Amen.

Faith and Provision

Operating within Kingdom economics requires faith. The world teaches self-reliance, but the Bible instructs us to rely on God as our ultimate provider. Matthew 6:31-33 (NIV) encourages believers to prioritize God's kingdom, saying,

"So do not worry, saying, 'What shall we eat?' or 'What shall we drink?' or 'What shall we wear?'... But seek first his kingdom and his righteousness, and all these things will be given to you as well."

There was a season in my life when I had more bills than income and no clear solution in sight. Every instinct told me to hustle harder, to make something happen on my own. But in prayer, God kept whispering, "Trust Me." So instead of panicking, I leaned into seeking Him more — spending time in worship, fasting, and studying His Word. I prioritized His presence over my problems. Slowly but surely, doors began to open — unexpected checks, new job offers, and favor I couldn't have orchestrated on my own. I realized then that when we truly seek God's kingdom first, He faithfully provides everything we need — often in ways that remind us it was never about our striving but about His goodness.

Let's Pray: Father, thank You for being our faithful provider. Help us to trust You more than we trust our own efforts. Teach us to seek You first, believing that as we prioritize Your kingdom, You will meet every need. Strengthen our faith to rest in Your promises and not to worry about tomorrow.

Daily Prayer Points for claiming your financial freedom and prosperity:

- Thank you God for giving me the authority to possess my financial possessions in the name of Jesus name.

- Oh God arise and change my financial status by fire in the name of Jesus.

- Oh God arise and have mercy on me.

- Every ancestral blockage to my finances scatter in the name of Jesus.

- Every demonic hold over my finances scatter in the name of Jesus.

- Oh God arise and let the story of my financial life change in Jesus name.

- Every evil power of my mother's house blocking my finances be destroyed in the name of Jesus.

- Every evil power of my father's house blocking my finances be destroyed in the name of Jesus.

- Holy Ghost magnetized my Divine prosperity to me in the name of Jesus.

- Every Power that is hindering my financial progress be dismantled in Jesus name.

Welcome to Your New Normal! Enjoy your life as you experience the transformational power of Kingdom Wealth. Be relentless to learn from your past, never live in it unless it brings you joy. This is your new beginning ordained by God through His Word! He said, "Beloved, I wish above all things that thou mayest prosper and be in health, even as thy soul prospereth" (3 John 2 NIV). So, remain in God and enjoy every gift and every promise He has placed in your today and in your future.

.

CHAPTER 6

THE REVELATION OF A WORTHY WOMAN

WRITTEN BY JESSICA HARRIS

It all begins...

Embarking on the journey of life transformation is no small feat. It requires courage to confront the depths of your limitations, rise from the pit of discouragement, and break free from years of just existing rather than thriving. But here's a foundational truth that underpins this journey: You are worth it.

I didn't always believe this for myself. For years, I lived in a constant battle with my body image. Every glance in the mirror was a critique, every meal a negotiation, and every day a struggle to feel "good enough." I tied my worth to the number on the scale, the size of my jeans, and the approval of others. No matter how much weight I lost or how perfect I tried to appear, I couldn't shake the gnawing doubt that I wasn't enough.

This constant self-judgment seeped into every part of my life. I questioned my abilities, doubted my value, and overcompensated by striving for perfection in everything I did. I thought if I could just fix my body, I'd fix my life. But that was a lie. Even when I reached physical goals, the emptiness inside remained. The truth is, I had abandoned myself. I had bought into the world's lie that my worth was tied to how I looked and what I achieved.

It wasn't until I hit rock bottom emotionally, spiritually, and physically that I realized the root of my struggle wasn't my body; it was my perception of my worth. I had placed my value in fleeting, external things and neglected the deeper truth of who I was in God.

Psalm 139:14 (NIV) began to take root in my heart: *"I praise You because I am fearfully and wonderfully made; Your works are wonderful, I know that full well."* Slowly, I started to see that my worth wasn't something I had to earn or prove it was inherent, given by God.

When I embraced this truth, everything began to change. I stopped seeing my body as a project to perfect and started viewing it as a gift to the steward. I stopped punishing myself for not being "enough" and started celebrating the unique person God created me to be.

The journey wasn't easy. Body image struggles don't disappear overnight, and self-doubt doesn't evaporate with a single revelation. But with each step, I learned to silence the lies and replace them with God's truth. I learned to take care of my body out of love, not fear. I learned to set boundaries and prioritize my needs without guilt. And most importantly, I learned to root my worth in who God says I am, not in what the world says I should be.

As I've guided hundreds of women through their own transformations, I've seen this same struggle play out time and time again. Women who feel trapped by the lie that their value depends on their appearance, achievements, or ability to please others. Women who long for change but don't believe they are worthy of it.

But here's the truth: You are not your body. You are not your mistakes. You are not your failures. Your worth is not tied to how you look, what you've done, or what others think of you. Your worth is rooted in God's unchanging love and the unique purpose He has for your life.

Romans 8:38-39 (NIV) declares, "For I am convinced that neither death nor life, neither angels nor demons, neither the present nor the future, nor any powers, neither height nor depth, nor anything else in all creation, will be able to separate us from the love of God that is in Christ Jesus our Lord."

If you've ever felt trapped by body image struggles or doubted your self-worth, I want you to know you are not alone. I've been there. I've felt the weight of those lies. But I've also seen the freedom that comes from stepping into God's truth.

Transformation isn't just about losing weight or changing habits, it's about reclaiming your God-given identity. It's about silencing the voice of self-doubt and embracing the truth that you are wonderfully made, deeply loved, and endlessly valuable.

So, let me ask you: Do you believe you are worth it? Do you believe you are worthy of the peace, joy, and freedom God has for you? Because when you begin to see yourself as God sees you, everything changes. The lies lose their power, and you step into the abundant life He has called you to live.

This is where your journey begins not with striving, but with believing. Believing you are enough. Believing you are worthy. Believing that with God, transformation is not only possible but promised. "And we know that in all things God works for the good of those who love Him, who have been called according to His purpose" (Romans 8:28 NIV). You are worth the effort. You are worth the investment. And you are worth the life God has waiting for you.

A Woman's Worth

In a world that places so much emphasis on external beauty, fleeting trends, and impossible standards, I've often felt like I was fighting an uphill battle. Like many women, I tied my worth to the reflection in the mirror and the opinions of others. For years, I thought if I could just achieve the "perfect" look or meet the world's expectations, I'd finally feel valuable.

I remember standing in front of the mirror, fixated on every perceived flaw, every imperfection. My self-talk was harsh, critical, and unforgiving. If only I were thinner. If only I were flawless. If only I could be someone else. These thoughts weren't fleeting; they became my constant companions, shaping how I viewed myself and lived my life.

What I didn't realize was how much I had allowed the world's lies to define me. Lies that whispered I needed to be more, do more, and look better to have worth. Lies that kept me in a cycle of comparison, striving, and exhaustion. Lies that left me feeling like I'd never be enough.

But God had a different story for me.

One day, in the middle of my self-doubt and striving, I came across a verse that stopped me in my tracks: "You are precious and honored in my sight, and I love you" (Isaiah 43:4 NIV). Precious. Honored. Loved. These were not words I had ever used to describe myself. Yet, here was God, speaking them over me.

For the first time, I began to see myself through God's eyes. He didn't see the flaws I obsessed over. He didn't measure my worth by my accomplishments, my appearance, or my failures. He saw me as His masterpiece, created with intention and purpose. "For we are God's handiwork, created in Christ Jesus to do good works, which God prepared in advance for us to do" (Ephesians 2:10 NIV).

That truth began to unravel the lies I had believed for so long. Slowly, I started to shift my focus. Instead of criticizing my body, I began to see it as a gift to steward. Instead of chasing external validation, I turned my attention to God's approval, which I already had. And instead of striving to be someone else, I leaned into the truth that I was fearfully and wonderfully made.

Proverbs 31 became a powerful reminder for me during this season. The woman described in this passage wasn't praised for her beauty or her accomplishments. Her worth came from her faith, strength, and character qualities that reflected her deep relationship with God.

"Charm is deceptive, and beauty is fleeting; but a woman who fears the Lord is to be praised." (Proverbs 31:30).

This was the kind of worth I wanted to embrace. A worth that wasn't tied to the trends of the world but to the eternal truth of who God says I am. The journey wasn't easy. The world's messages didn't disappear overnight, and my inner critic didn't go silent immediately. There were days when the lies still felt louder than the truth. But with every step, I began to reclaim my identity as a daughter of God.

This transformation didn't just change how I saw myself, it changed how I lived my life. When I embraced my worth:

- I stopped comparing myself to others and began celebrating the unique person God created me to be.
- I set boundaries in relationships that drained me and started prioritizing what truly mattered.
- I pursued my God-given purpose with confidence and intention, no longer held back by fear or insecurity.

Now, when I look in the mirror, I don't see perfection, but I do see someone who is deeply loved and valued by God. I see a woman who is not defined by the world's standards but by her Creator, and that has made all the difference.

The same is true for you. If you've ever felt like you're not enough or believed the lies of the world, I want you to know this: You are precious, honored, and loved. Your worth is not something you have to earn or prove; it's something you already have because of who God is and who He created you to be.

Imagine standing in front of the mirror and seeing yourself as God sees you. He looks at you with love, pride, and delight. You are His daughter, His masterpiece, and nothing can change that.

"The King is enthralled by your beauty; honor Him, for He is your Lord." (Psalm 45:11 NIV).

So, let me ask you: What lies about your worth have you believed? How might your life change if you embraced your God-given identity? This is your invitation to let go of the lies, the striving, and the self-doubt. To reclaim your worth and step into the life God has called you to live. A life of confidence, purpose, and freedom. You are precious. You are loved. You are enough.

"She is clothed with strength and dignity; she can laugh at the days to come." (Proverbs 31:25 NIV).

This is where your story begins not with striving, but with believing. Believing you are worthy, not because of what you do or how you look, but because of who you are in Him. And that, dear reader, is a life worth embracing.

Conscious Consumption: What's Eating You?

For years, I thought my struggles with food were about willpower. I convinced myself that if I could just stick to the perfect plan, follow the latest diet, or resist temptation a little harder, everything would fall into place. But no matter how many times I started over, I always ended up back at the same place frustrated, defeated, and stuck. What I didn't realize then was that food wasn't the real problem. It wasn't about what I was eating; it was about what was eating me.

I can vividly remember one evening when everything came to a head. I was standing in my kitchen after a particularly stressful day, staring at the empty wrappers of the snacks I had mindlessly devoured. I wasn't even hungry, but something inside me was aching. I was stressed, lonely, and overwhelmed, and food had become my go-to comfort, my escape.

But as I stood there, I realized something profound: the food wasn't fixing anything. If anything, it was only adding to my guilt and shame. I wasn't feeding my body; I was trying to feed my emotions.

That moment was a turning point for me. I realized I needed to take a deeper look at my relationship with food and with myself. What was I really hungry for? What was driving me to use food as a bandage for my emotions? And most importantly, how could I break free from this cycle?

The Deeper Hunger

As I began to dig into these questions, I discovered a truth that changed everything: emotional eating isn't about food it's about what's happening beneath the surface. Stress, loneliness, shame, fear these are the real culprits, the things that drive us to use food as a way to cope.

But food can never satisfy that kind of hunger. Jesus said, "I am the bread of life. Whoever comes to me will never go hungry, and whoever believes in me will never be thirsty." (John 6:35 NIV). For the first time, I understood that the emptiness I felt wasn't something food could fill. Only God could meet that deeper need.

This realization didn't make the journey easy, but it gave me clarity. I started paying attention to my patterns, asking myself tough questions, and inviting God into the process. And as I did, I began to see food differently not as a source of comfort or control, but as a gift meant to nourish my body and honor the One who created it.

Wake Up and Read the Label

One of the first practical changes I made was becoming more intentional about what I was eating. I started reading labels, choosing foods that were as close to their natural state as possible, and avoiding the overly processed, artificial options I had relied on for so long.

It wasn't just about eating "clean" or following another set of rules, it was about waking up to the truth. God created food to nourish us, not to confuse or harm us. When I read 1 Corinthians 10:31 (NIV) "So whether you eat or drink or whatever you do, do it all for the glory of God" I realized I hadn't been honoring God in the way I was nourishing my body. Real food doesn't need a list of unpronounceable ingredients or flashy marketing. My body, fearfully and wonderfully made, deserved to be fed with care and intention.

Breaking the Cycle

But mindful eating was only part of the journey. The deeper work was learning to deal with the emotional triggers that drove me to food in the first place. It wasn't easy. There were days I wanted to give up, times when I slipped back into old habits. But with every step, I learned to recognize the patterns and replace them with healthier choices.

Here's what helped me break the cycle:

1. Recognize the Trigger:
When I felt the urge to eat, I started pausing to ask myself, Am I really hungry, or is this an emotional trigger? Naming the emotion; whether it was stress, boredom, or sadness; helped me address the real issue instead of masking it with food.

2. Turn to God:
Instead of running to the pantry, I began running to God. I poured out my feelings in prayer, asking Him to meet my needs and fill the voids in my heart. Philippians 4:6-7 (NIV) became my anchor: *"Do not be anxious about anything, but in every situation, by prayer and petition, with thanksgiving, present your requests to God. And the peace of God, which transcends all understanding, will guard your hearts and your minds in Christ Jesus."*

3. Eat With Intention:
I slowed down during meals, eliminating distractions and truly savoring each bite. This helped me listen to my body's cues and stop eating when I was satisfied.

4. Prepare for Greater:
I realized that emotional eating often struck when I was unprepared. By planning meals and snacks ahead of time, I set myself up for success instead of relying on convenience foods.

5. Extend Grace to Myself:
Healing isn't linear. There were times I stumbled, but I learned to offer myself grace and keep moving forward. God's love for me wasn't dependent on my performance, and that truth gave me the freedom to grow without shame.

Transformation Through Conscious Choices

As I embraced these changes, I began to see food and myself differently. My relationship with food became less about control and more about care. My body, once a source of frustration and shame, became something I wanted to honor and nurture.

This journey also deepened my faith. I realized that God cares about every part of our lives, including what we eat. When we invite Him into this area, He brings healing, freedom, and peace.

Your Next Step

If you're feeling stuck in your relationship with food, I want you to know you're not alone. I've been there. I've felt the frustration, the guilt, and the hopelessness. But I've also seen what's possible when you take a step back and address the deeper issues. Ask yourself:

What's eating you?

What emotions or struggles are you trying to feed with food? How can you invite God into your relationship with eating and begin to find freedom?

You don't have to have it all figured out today. Start small. Take one step. Trust that God will meet you where you are and guide you toward healing. Remember, this isn't about perfection it's about intention. And as you make conscious choices, you'll discover a life that's not just free from the chains of emotional eating, but also filled with the peace and satisfaction that only God can provide.

You are worth the effort. Your healing is worth the journey. And with God's help, you can break free and step into the life He's calling you to live.

CHAPTER 7

A TOTAL TRANSFORMATION

WRITTEN BY MYASIA OBAZEE

Part 1: The Unveiling

holding to the outward form of godliness but denying its power.
Avoid them!
2 Timothy 3:5 (NRSVUE)

There are many people in the Body of Christ who believe within their heart that there is more for them in their faith journey or that God Himself is requiring more of them, simply put. They have gotten accustomed to the scheduled tasks and the routine life of work, life, and/or church, yet something on the inside of them is yearning for more. However, identifying what 'it' may be can be a challenge depending on where you are in your walk with God.

As for me, the first time I knew I desired more in my faith journey was in 2016, when I was about 3 years into my walk with God. During a group bible discussion, we were all asked the question, "What do you desire in this season of your life?" My response was, "Intimacy with God!" It came to my mind so clearly. Although I had no idea that God was speaking to my heart at the time, it was truly my heart's desire. The only problem was, at that time:

(1) I didn't fully understand what 'intimacy with God' meant,
(2) I didn't have a relationship with God,
(3) I didn't have the faith to believe God could speak to me.

Now you may be reading this, asking, "How in the world can you believe in Christ and not know these things? Unfortunately, I was in a religious cult that had a form of godliness but denied the power thereof. In 2012-2013, I was seeking God and was introduced to love bombing, gaslighting, manipulation, and control.

These were many red flags that I ignored because the spirit of rejection in me wanted to belong. So I joined, and after a few years, I realized I wanted more. God, in His infinite wisdom, answered me after six and a half years, and for that, I am grateful.

because no prophecy ever came by human will, but men and women moved by the Holy Spirit spoke from God.
2 Peter 1:21 (NRSVUE)

After being stuck in the cycle of a religious system for six and a half years, God finally got my attention. Looking back, I know it was only the grace and mercy of God that kept me from losing my mind at a greater capacity. It was by His divine orchestration that breaking free a cult religion, had come to an end. After declaring that I wanted to grow in my intimacy with God over the next two years, I began religiously fasting the first 8 days of each month. The focus was just to pray and ask God for clarity about many life decisions I needed to make. Everything seemed to be going as I would have planned and hoped until one day, while at an event, I encountered a prophet. Things were said about my life and spoken into my life that only God knew about. I truly believe that is when the shift began.

As the next monthly fast came around, my focus was to ask God for clarity on my plans, but I felt this strong urgency to study the Holy Spirit instead. For me, being this intentional was new and refreshing because I did not know much about the Holy Spirit. I was looking forward to learning outside of what teaching I was fed in the religious cult. As my life began to shift, I began to seek God about the power and authority I saw in the prophet who spoke into my life. I wanted more of God, and He reminded me of my prayer discovering the 'intimacy with God' was finally coming to pass.

"If you, then, who are evil, know how to give good gifts to your children, how much more will the heavenly Father give the Holy Spirit[a] to those who ask him!" Luke 11:13 (NRSVUE)

As I began to read more about the Holy Spirit and God's word, I felt opposition. I would read the word and hear in my mind, "that's not true," or "that doesn't exist anymore". I continued to pray, and the Holy Spirit began to teach me about the error of teaching I received. I was given the wisdom and instruction to renounce, unlearn, and apply the truth of God's word over my mind and my life. Soon after, the Holy Spirit told me my time in the religious cult was up and to part ways. When I finally met with the leadership of that church about why I was leaving; I was told, "You're going down a dark, destructive path". Regardless of the backlash I received, I continued to obey God.

As I grew in my understanding of God's word, my prayers began to shift. I started to ask God for the very thing I said I didn't believe in, "The Baptism of the Holy Spirit because I knew that in order for me to keep growing in my intimacy with God, I needed Him in a greater way." I realized that it was not enough to just simply accept Christ as Lord (Romans 10:9, *NRSVUE*) or repent and be baptized (Acts 2:38 *NRSVUE*), but we need to be born again (John 3:3 *NRSVUE*) of water and the Spirit of God.

"Jesus answered him, "Very truly, I tell you, no one can see the kingdom of God without being born from above."[b] 4 Nicodemus said to him, "How can anyone be born after having grown old? Can one enter a second time into the mother's womb and be born?" 5 Jesus answered, "Very truly, I tell you, no one can enter the kingdom of God without being born of water and Spirit. 6 What is born of the flesh is flesh, and what is born of the Spirit is spirit." John 3:3-6 (NRSVUE)

As I began praying to be born again, I didn't fully understand what I was asking for, but I knew that for me to live in the fullness of God, I needed more of Him and less of me. God began to reveal how much of my life I had control over and the true revelation behind denying myself, picking up my cross, and following Christ. I went through a process God correcting every false teaching so that I could receive the fullness of God I was searching for. God told me He needed me to be open, yielded, and ready to surrender my life to Him. He emphasized that if I had any hindrances, it could prevent His Holy Spirit from dwelling inside of me. He revealed that my unbelief, doubt, fears, and unforgiveness were all hindering me from moving forward in this newfound hope in God. He was breaking the spirit of religion off of me and humbled me as my prayer became not my will, but His will be done. I began to accept the fact that receiving the promises of God were yes and amen, but with the proper heart posture.

"Keep on asking, and you will receive what you ask for. Keep on seeking, and you will find. Keep on knocking, and the door will be opened to you. 8 For everyone who asks receives. Everyone who seeks finds. And to everyone who knocks, the door will be opened." Matthew 7:7-8 (NRSVUE)

I continued to pray and ask God for the Baptism of the Holy Spirit because I finally discovered why I needed His Holy Spirit. I no longer wanted to live my life in my own strength, I needed help in overcoming many struggles, and I truly wanted to walk in the purpose God had ordained for me. There were times I got sad, frustrated, and weary because what I was praying for was not happening when I thought it would, but I stayed consistent. Days leading up to being baptized in the Holy Spirit, He gave me a dream, and I could audibly hear myself speaking in a language I didn't understand. He then gave me another dream and told me who He was calling me to be. God told me great and mighty things, and my heart was finally open to receive fully.

While staying with them, he ordered them not to leave Jerusalem but to wait there for the promise of the Father. "This," he said, "is what you have heard from me; for John baptized with water, but you will be baptized with the Holy Spirit not many days from now. But you will receive power when the Holy Spirit has come upon you, and you will be my witnesses in Jerusalem, in all Judea and Samaria, and to the ends of the earth." Acts 1:4-5;8 (NRSVUE)

I went from asking for the baptism of the Holy Spirit to thanking God in faith that I already had it, and in January 2020, I was baptized in the Holy Spirit. Naturally speaking, it appeared as though my life flipped upside down. My business dried up, and so much was happening in my life, but spiritually, I was in alignment. For six weeks straight, God sent His prophets to tell me God was changing my address, calling me to ministry, and that I had a call on my life. By March 2020, the world had shut down, and by April, I was on a one-way flight to Houston, Texas. I came to this new place with all that I knew but had no idea life would never be the same.

Part II. The Transformation

Do not conform to the pattern of this world but be transformed by the renewing of your mind. Then you will be able to test and approve what God's will is his good, pleasing, and perfect will. Romans 12:1-2 (NRSVUE)

If you had the mindset I had as a young 30-year-old, you most likely ran away from what was required of you to get to where God needed you to be, unknowingly. Or maybe you didn't run away; however, navigating to get there can seem impossible. These are just indicators that your mind must be renewed with the truth that comes to set us free. Why? Well, the giant in front of you may be speaking more than the voice of God. The truth of the matter is that God is looking for ways to show us His word won't return to Him void. He is the same yesterday, today, and forever more.

We read in the word of God that He is Jehovah Jireh, "The Lord who provides" (Genesis 22:14), Jehovah Rapha, "The Lord who Heals" (Exodus 15:26), and El Roi, " The God who Sees me" (Genesis 16:13). These were all pivotal moments in my transformation I was able to witness beyond reading it in the word of God. Because God is a Man of His word and faithful to perform what He said He would do, He is looking for us to position ourselves to receive His promises which are yes and amen (Hebrews 10:23, Philippians 1:6, 2 Corinthians 1:20)

Before we receive the promises of God, there is a posture we must take. After sharing with you some of my backstory of what it took to transition to a new place, I want to take you on my journey of God transforming my life and how these key tools can help you as you navigate the next seasons in your own life as well.

Build Your Faith

"Faith comes by hearing and hearing the word of God." Romans 10:17 (NRSVUE)

"Then Jesus was led up by the spirit into the wilderness to be tempted by the devil. 2 and after he had fasted for forty days and forty nights, he [a]then became hungry. 3 and the tempter came and said to him, "If you are the son of god, command that these stones become bread." 4 but he answered and said, "it is written: 'man shall not live on bread alone, but on every word that comes out of the mouth of god." Matthew 4:1-11 (NRSVUE)

When I think about the process God took me through, I can only thank God for His grace to endure the journey to be where I am today. As believers, we all must be processed to get to the place where we can be who God has called us to be. A process is a series of actions or steps taken to achieve a particular end. The wilderness is one of the places we must go through to get to the Promised Land.

When you hear the word 'process,' what are the first few thoughts that come to your mind? Maybe you're thinking: How Long is this going to take? Or You don't have it in you to wait!" No matter what your thoughts are, the truth is your faith must come from what the Holy Spirit has said, according to the word of God. "Faith comes by hearing and hearing the word of God (Romans 10:17 *NRSVUE*)." As you journey through the wilderness, your faith will be tested, as you are tempted by the enemy so that God can see where your faith is.

When Jesus was led into the wilderness by the Spirit of God, it revealed who Jesus relied on when He was being tempted by the enemy in His mind. The beautiful truth is that nothing happens without God's permission. "My sheep hear my voice and a stranger's voice they won't follow,"(John 10:27) and Jesus showed what it meant to hear God speak and then declare what God had spoken. He was full of the word. On your journey through this life, it is your faith that needs to be built on God's word alone. Not the opinions of man, not what your family thinks, or those closest to you. At the end of the day, God's word never returns back void, so when you declare it in the atmosphere of faith, it will do what it was intended to do according to God's will.

Renew your mind

Let this mind be in you, which was also in Christ Jesus Philippians 2:5 (NRSVUE)

When we make Jesus savior and Lord of our lives, there are many seasons of unlearning and relearning. From unlearning thought patterns, traditions of men, church culture, false doctrine, or just habits that don't align with the character of Christ or the nature of God. If we are honest, when we come to know something new, we attempt to make the new things fit in our lives, hoping all will be well. But in God, the reality is there are many things we must give up in order to receive the fullness of God.

The mind is the place God desires to have full control. It's the place where He speaks audibly, even visually. It's one of the places where we can worship God in Spirit and Truth. The problem is that satan attacks the mind, and in order to overcome the enemy, we must come out of agreement with the lies, and take hold of the truth, and declare what the Lord has said.

"for the weapons of our warfare are not merely human,[a] but they have divine power to destroy strongholds. We destroy arguments 5 and every proud obstacle raised up against the knowledge of God, and we take every thought captive to obey Christ." 2 Corinthians 10:4-5 (NRSVUE)

This scripture tells us that the weapons that we use to fight our spiritual battles are not human weapons but weapons God gives us. We are to use these weapons to knock down the strongholds of our human reasoning and destroy every false argument. We are to destroy proud obstacles that hinder us or others from knowing God. God tells us to capture the rebellious thoughts and teach them to obey or submit to Christ. In the process of being transformed, making a conscience decision to renew your mind is one of the most important things you, as a believer, can do in your walk with God. It is one of the practical strategies I share with believers as they walk out their deliverance.

Walk out your Deliverance.

"If you abide in me and my words abide in you, ask for whatever you wish, and it will be done for you." John 15:7 (NRSVUE)

"When the righteous cry for help, the Lord hears and delivers them out of all their troubles." Psalm 34:17 (NRSVUE)

Walking out your deliverance is truly a journey. It takes prayer, the word of God, fasting, patience, faith, having the right heart posture, and support, just to name a few. Deliverance is not a one-size-fits-all, however, there are some things that remain true; when we humble ourselves before God and cry out for help, God will deliver us from what troubles us. Deliverance also won't happen the way we think it will happen in our logical minds. Many times, people become more focused on the videos they see online, the stories they read in books, or the testimonies of others and begin to imagine or believe that's how God will do it for them. The issue here is that you can miss God simply because you've unknowingly put an Omnipresent (All seeing), Omniscient (All Knowing), Omnipotent (All Powerful) God inside of a box He doesn't belong in.

Unlearning & Relearning

Now this I affirm and insist on in the Lord: you must no longer walk as the gentiles walk, in the futility of their minds; 18 they are darkened in their understanding, alienated from the life of God because of their ignorance and hardness of heart. 19 They have lost all sensitivity and have abandoned themselves to licentiousness, greedy to practice every kind of impurity. 20 That is not the way you learned Christ! 21 For surely you have heard about him and were taught in him, as truth is in Jesus, 22 to put away your former way of life, your old self, corrupt and deluded by its lusts, 23 and to be renewed in the spirit of your minds, 24 and to clothe yourselves with the new self, created according to the likeness of God in true righteousness and holiness. Ephesians 4:17-24 (NRSVUE)

As you walk out your deliverance, God will make clear things that are not His will for you. If it goes against His nature and Christ's likeness, more than likely, you'll have to give It up. Yes, God is full of grace and patience, but His goal is to see us all come to a place of repentance (2 Peter 3:9) so that we don't perish.

The unlearning and relearning process is continual as a believer, so remaining humble and teachable is a must. Remember, during seasons of deliverance we are simply putting off the old man and putting on the new nature of Christ. Just like a child can learn how to talk, respond, play, and act at home, once they go to school, they become exposed to a new environment, and when they go back home, they have to unlearn certain behaviors that may not work at home, My encouragement to anyone seeking deliverance would be to let God have His way, and each day on your journey, surrender your will, yield to His way, and have an open heart to receive. Don't forget God is rewriting your story.

Thrive in God

"For surely I know the plans I have for you, says the Lord, plans for your welfare and not for harm, to give you a future with hope." Jeremiah 29:11 (NRSVUE)

"The earth is the Lord's and all that is in it, the world, and those who live in it, for he has founded it on the seas and established it on the rivers." Psalms 23:1-3 (NRSVUE)

"Beloved, I pray that all may go well with you and that you may be in good health, as it goes well with your soul." 3 John 1:2 (NRSVUE)

Spiritually being aligned with God is the best way to live. Before God can bless us, He must clean us up so that we don't sabotage the increase. Before God can elevate us, we must get to a place of stewarding well what is in our care. God desires that we thrive in every area of our lives, mentally, emotionally, physically, and spiritually. We cannot despise the small beginnings but keep a heart of gratitude as we grow in God.

One of the many ways you know you are thriving in God is the production of fruit that comes from it. This isn't to say that bad fruit or rotten fruit won't come because discerning what season you are in is also important. When we realize bad fruit, bad habits, or tendencies, God prunes those areas so they don't affect other areas in our lives. When you prematurely move into a season God has not graced you to be in, you run the risk of not being effective and losing.

Your lifestyle, your character, your decision-making, your stewardship, and how you execute what God has entrusted you with all play a key role in how you thrive in God. God promises that when you are faithful over the little, He will give you more (Matthew 25:23). As believers, we are called to be lenders and now borrowers (Psalms 15:5), the head and not the tail, above and not beneath (Deuteronomy 28:13). So as we thrive in God, we set ourselves up to help others in their journey so they can do the same.

"Whatever you do, work heartily, as for the Lord and not for men, knowing that from the Lord you will receive the inheritance as your reward. You are serving the Lord Christ." Colossians 3:23-24 (NRSVUE)

Above all else, as you thrive in God, remember that the end goal is for God to be glorified and for others to know who Christ is. Let your light shine before men so that they see your good deeds and glorify God in heaven (Matthew 5:14). My prayer is that you allow the Spirit of God to do the work in you and bring it to completion (Philippians 1:6) so that you can truly be all that He has called you to be before the foundation of this world.

ABOUT THE AUTHORS

@moniquelovel   f @moniquelovel   ✉ pivotalimpactcc@gmail.com   🌐 moniquelovel.com

Monique McCray

LIFE STRATEGIST AND PURPOSE DEVELOPMENT COACH
SOCIAL WORKER AND BOARD-CERTIFIED CHRISTIAN COUNSELOR

ABOUT ME

Monique Loviel is a dedicated Christian Strategy Coach and Counselor with a background in social work and counseling, specializing in helping individuals who are transitioning or feeling stuck in a place of stagnation. Through her training in TF-CBT, Narrative Therapy, and Solution-Focused Brief Therapy, Monique blends evidence-based therapeutic techniques with faith-centered coaching to create personalized life strategies. She empowers clients to break through emotional barriers, navigate life transitions, and align with their divine purpose, guiding them toward healing, growth, and renewed clarity in both their personal and spiritual lives.

PIVOTAL IMPACT COUNSELING AND CONSULTING, LLC

Pivotal Impact helps individuals achieve personal, emotional, and spiritual growth through a faith-based approach that combines biblical principles with proven coaching and counseling techniques to navigate challenges, deepen their relationship with God, and align with their divine purpose.

Coaching Program or Services Offered:
Counseling, Life Strategy Coaching, Support Group, Discipleship and Ministry Development Coaching, LauncHer and Maximiz(H}er, Nonprofit

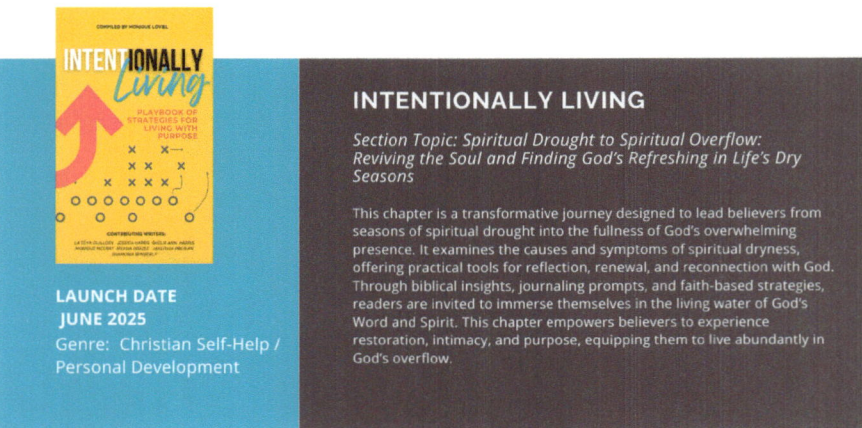

LAUNCH DATE
JUNE 2025
Genre: Christian Self-Help /
Personal Development

INTENTIONALLY LIVING

Section Topic: Spiritual Drought to Spiritual Overflow: Reviving the Soul and Finding God's Refreshing in Life's Dry Seasons

This chapter is a transformative journey designed to lead believers from seasons of spiritual drought into the fullness of God's overwhelming presence. It examines the causes and symptoms of spiritual dryness, offering practical tools for reflection, renewal, and reconnection with God. Through biblical insights, journaling prompts, and faith-based strategies, readers are invited to immerse themselves in the living water of God's Word and Spirit. This chapter empowers believers to experience restoration, intimacy, and purpose, equipping them to live abundantly in God's overflow.

@i_am_latoya_guillory   info@empowered-with-purpose.net   1-337-257-0701   empowered-with-purpose.net

La'Toya Guillory
AUTHOR AND MINDSET COACH

ABOUT ME

I have had the privilege of calling Lafayette, Louisiana, my home for over two decades; with a strong background in the social service field, I have witnessed firsthand the impact of individuals who long to know and understand who they are.

My unique coaching style inspires and empowers individuals to live authentically within the purpose that they believe God has set out for them. As the owner of Empowered with Purpose LLC, I passionately lead my community toward their own empowerment by teaching them to write their own stories.

I am the published author of five books, including Anchored in Christ, which includes a study guide and three journals: The Purposely Driven Journal, The Empower You Journal, and The Unshakeable Marriage Journal.

In addition to my writings, I am the host and producer of "The Purposely Driven Podcast," a platform accessible on all major podcast platforms. You can easily find my books on popular retail platforms like Amazon, Books A Million, Barnes and Noble, and within the Acadiana area. In 2023 I took the lead in organizing the inaugural Black Author Expo. The Black Author Expo gave me a vision to create a vibrant community among local authors and creative individuals driven by a passion for creating their own narratives.

EMPOWERED WITH PURPOSE, LLC

My approach to coaching is rooted in positive and emotional intelligence, and mindfulness. I work collaboratively with my clients to help them identify their strengths, overcome limiting beliefs, and develop practical strategies for achieving their writing goals.

Coaching Program or Services Offered:

Mindset Coaching, Author Coaching, Anthology Coaching, online courses, copy editing, proofreading, self-publishing assistance, and audio narration

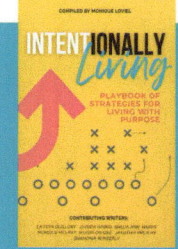

LAUNCH DATE
JUNE 2025
Genre: Christian Self-Help / Personal Development

INTENTIONALLY LIVING

Section Topic: Relationship Resiliency / Building and Sustaining Meaningful Relationships

The author guides readers on living with purpose and resilience through biblical stories of transformation. "Own Your Truth" explores coping with loss and trauma, drawing from Naomi's journey of grief and perseverance. "You Have an Assignment" highlights David's commitment to his calling, emphasizing emotional boundaries and focus. "Your Value Unveiled" reflects on the Prodigal Son's path to rediscovering identity and worth despite setbacks. Lastly, "Kingdom Confidence" shows Esther's courage in fulfilling her mission, balancing loyalty with purpose and overcoming self-doubt. Together, these stories provide practical insights and exercises to help readers live intentionally with faith and confidence.

OTHER PUBLISHED WORKS: Anchored Book and Study Guide
The Empowered You (Journal)
Unshakeable Marriage (Journal)
Purposely Driven (Journal)
Purposely Driven Podcast

@iliveonpurpose f @sheliasimmons35 ✉ singleconnectcoaching@gmail.com 🌐 singleconnectcoaching.square.site

Shelia Ann Harris

PURPOSED COACH, MINISTER, AUTHOR, PODCASTER, AND PHOTOGRAPHER

ABOUT ME

Shelia Harris is a minister of faith, photographer, sought-after MC, and host of the Let's Talk Kingdom Podcast. A writer and serial entrepreneur, Shelia released her first e-book, Leap of Faith, in 2021. Originally from Baton Rouge, Louisiana, she now lives in Houston, Texas, with her husband, Damien, their five children, and one grandchild. She is the founder of Singles-Connect Ministries, where she empowers believers in their faith journey. With a passion for service and community, Shelia continues to inspire and uplift others through her ministry, business ventures, and personal endeavors.

SINGLES-CONNECT

Singles-Connect Coaching helps believers deepen their relationship with Christ and prepare for Christ-centered relationships. The coaching focuses on spiritual growth, self-discovery, and emotional maturity, guiding individuals to align with God's purpose for their lives and relationships. The goal is to empower them to become whole, discern God's will, and live by biblical principles, ensuring they are spiritually and emotionally ready for fulfilling relationships.

Coaching Program or Services Offered:
Life Coaching, Discipleship Coaching, Purpose Development Coaching

LAUNCH DATE
JUNE 2025
Genre: Christian Self-Help / Personal Development

INTENTIONALLY LIVING

Section Topic: A Total Transformation

In this chapter, you'll discover that purpose isn't something distant or reserved for the extraordinary; it's already within you. God has purposed you, yes, even in the everyday. You'll be encouraged to see that your divine assignment may not always look the way you imagined, but it's perfectly aligned with who you are and who you are becoming. Through personal insight and spiritual truth, this chapter helps you recognize that purpose isn't just something you do; it's who you are. After reading, you'll walk away with a deeper understanding that Divine Purpose is not just a calling, it's your design.

OTHER PUBLISHED WORKS: Leap of Faith (Ebook)
Let's Talk Kingdom Podcast

R.E.S.E.T COACHING ,LLC.

Jakeithia's coaching approach focuses on empowering individuals to assess themselves by re-evaluating areas where growth is needed. She works collaboratively with her clients to help them overcome self-sabotage and imposter syndrome while nurturing self-love and personal worth.

Coaching Program or Services Offered:
R.E.S.E.T. Life Coaching and Writing Coaching

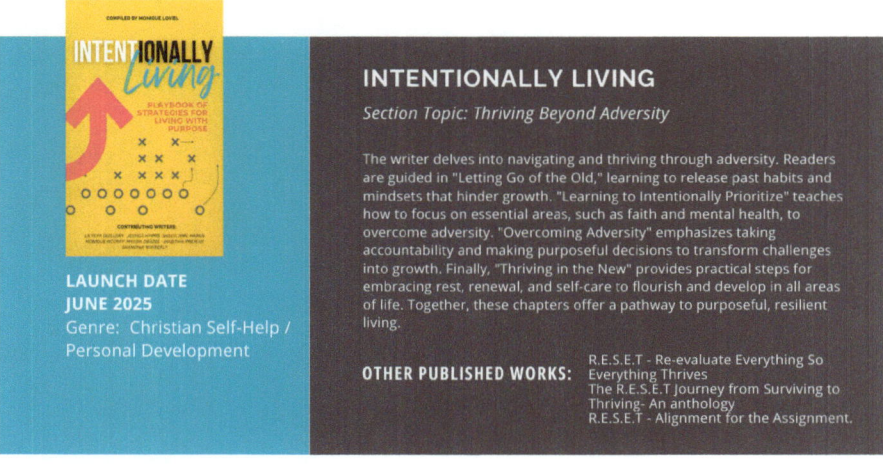

98

f @shamonia.wimberly   @shamoniawimberly   monawimberly@gmail.com   successstrategistinstitute.com

Dr. Shamonia Wimberly

LIFE COACH AND FINANCIAL COACH, SUCCESS STRATEGIST

ABOUT ME

Dr. Shamonia Wimberly is a leader at the intersection of faith and entrepreneurship. She is the founder of Dr. Shamonia Wimberly Ministries, creator of Shakyra Renee' Jewelry, and a key figure at the Success Strategist Institute. Combining her deep faith and life experiences, she empowers others through her jewelry business and financial expertise, helping them break free from struggles. Dr. Shamonia believes in the synergy between faith and entrepreneurship, encouraging bold action with scripture-based inspiration. She aspires to expand her ministry globally while continuing to serve and empower others through both her ministry and business.

SUCCESS STRATEGIST INSTITUTE

The Success Strategist Institute helps individuals and businesses achieve their goals through strategic guidance and personal empowerment. Focusing on leadership, goal setting, and business growth, it empowers clients to thrive professionally and personally with actionable plans and mentorship.

Coaching Program or Services Offered:
Life and Financial Coaching, Success Strategist, and Theological Studies

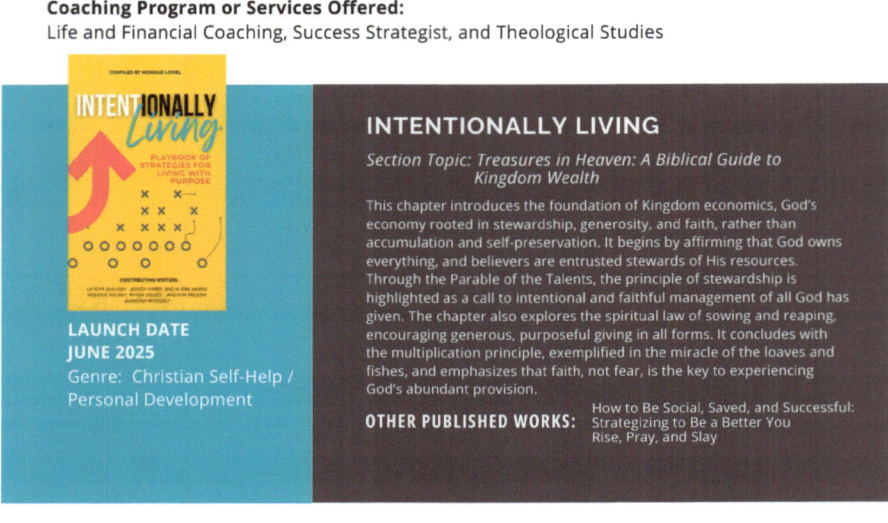

**LAUNCH DATE
JUNE 2025**
Genre: Christian Self-Help / Personal Development

INTENTIONALLY LIVING

Section Topic: Treasures in Heaven: A Biblical Guide to Kingdom Wealth

This chapter introduces the foundation of Kingdom economics, God's economy rooted in stewardship, generosity, and faith, rather than accumulation and self-preservation. It begins by affirming that God owns everything, and believers are entrusted stewards of His resources. Through the Parable of the Talents, the principle of stewardship is highlighted as a call to intentional and faithful management of all God has given. The chapter also explores the spiritual law of sowing and reaping, encouraging generous, purposeful giving in all forms. It concludes with the multiplication principle, exemplified in the miracle of the loaves and fishes, and emphasizes that faith, not fear, is the key to experiencing God's abundant provision.

OTHER PUBLISHED WORKS: How to Be Social, Saved, and Successful: Strategizing to Be a Better You
Rise, Pray, and Slay

@officiallyjessicaharris ⨍ officiallyJHarris ✉ jsmothersftwt@gmail.com 🌐 www.JESSICASMOTHERS.com

Jessica Harris

HEALTH AND WHOLENESS AMBASSADOR, AUTHOR, COACH

ABOUT ME

Jessica is a dynamic force in the realm of health and wellness. As a published author with a faith-based approach, Jessica is dedicated to a proactive change in the health and wellness landscape. As a Certified Health and Wellness Ambassador and Certified Fitness Trainer, Jessica is on a mission to activate the seat of destiny in every woman, building unstoppable momentum, unimaginable potential, and unquestionable worth in every season of life. In essence, it's about becoming whole.

THE WHOLE WOMAN CONSERVATORY

Jessica's coaching style is bold, holistic, and Kingdom-focused, designed to address every aspect of a woman's life. She understands that spirit, soul, and body are deeply interconnected, and true transformation requires alignment in every area.

Jessica's approach is not about temporary fixes; it's about equipping women with the tools to sustain wholeness and live with purpose.

Coaching Program or Services Offered: *Life Coaching, Health and Wellness Coaching*
Be Made Whole: 6-Week Signature Program
This program is a holistic journey designed to guide women toward becoming who they were created to be while actively pursuing wholeness in every season of life.

LAUNCH DATE
JUNE 2025

Genre: Christian Self-Help /
Personal Development

INTENTIONALLY LIVING

Section Topic: Revelation of a Worthy Woman

Jessica invites the reader on a heartfelt journey that isn't just about learning new truths it's about remembering what has always been true. She gently peels back the layers of lack of self worth, insecurity, and the lies the world has told, revealing the undeniable reality of a woman's worth.

This is more than an invitation; it's an awakening. Jessica invites readers to reconnect with the truth that their worth isn't earned through accomplishments, beauty, or approval. It's inherently placed within them by the creator. It's a mirror, reflecting the beauty and value you've always carried.

OTHER PUBLISHED WORKS: Deliver Me From Me

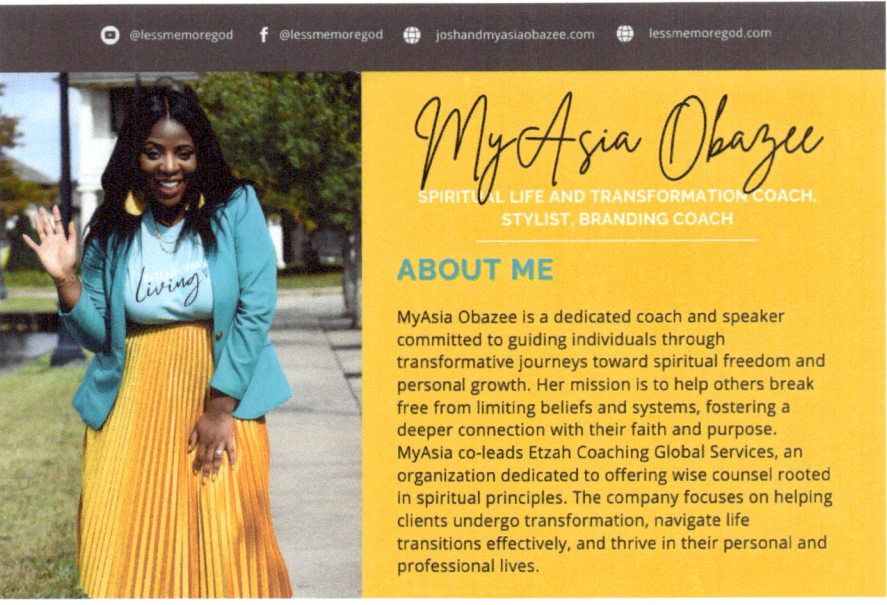

ETZAH COACHING GLOBAL SERVICES

Etzah Coaching Global Services employs a faith-based coaching approach, emphasizing the importance of spiritual growth and alignment. She combines personal testimony with biblical principles to create a supportive environment where clients can confront challenges, heal, and progress toward their goals.

Coaching Program or Services Offered:
Spiritual Deliverance, Breaking Free from Religious Systems, Renouncing Secret Societies

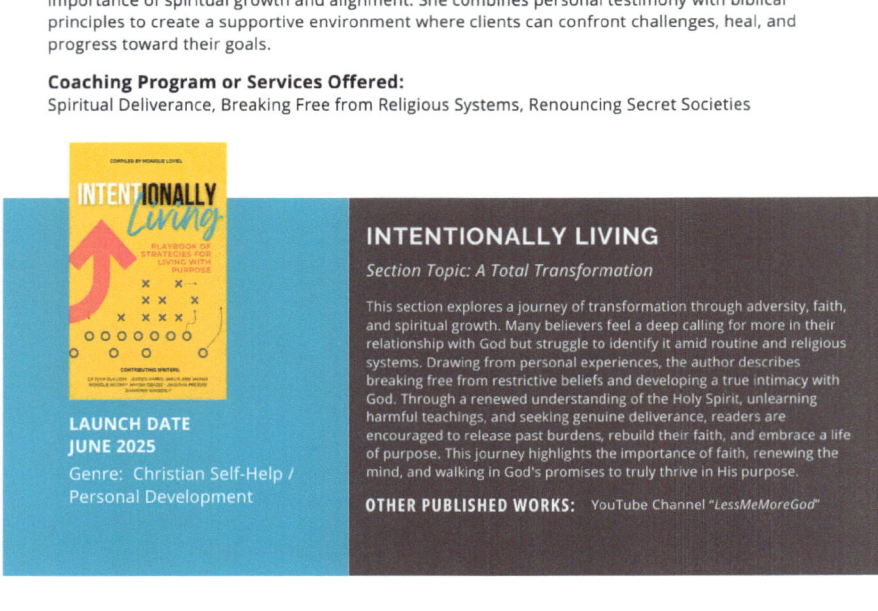

www.ingramcontent.com/pod-product-compliance
Lightning Source LLC
Chambersburg PA
CBHW040846120626
46547CB00001B/49